The Origin and [...]
- new Insights fr[om ... hyp]notic regressions into life between lives

James H. Burch

© James H. Burch

The cover is used here gratefully with permission of www.Freepik.com[1].

---

1. http://www.Freepik.com

Foreword

The inspiration for this book has been the decades-long, nearly 7,000-subject hypnotic regression sessions by Dr. Michael Newton, many of which were documented in two of his books written from the mid-1980s to the early 2000s titled *Journey of Souls* and *Destiny of Souls*. The titles may sound religious or spirituality-based, and they are to some degree. But he never claimed to be a priest or minister of any kind and never claimed to be writing theology or philosophy. He simply recounted what he found *to be*.

In fact, Dr. Michael Newton resisted any patients who came looking for past life regressions or anything to do with "past lives" for many years into his practice, explaining that he was a more traditional hypnotherapist. That was until he asked one patient to take him to the time and place of his pain. That changed everything.

Later in his life, Dr. Newton explained that he was always put off by both those who professed an overly fearful religious philosophy of life derived from adherence to most organized religions and also by atheists, whom he believed were themselves never quite satisfied with that view of existence. He thought there had to be an immense *purpose* to life. He credits his patients with pulling him, almost against his will, into a gradual realization of who we are, what we are doing here, and where we are going. Most of all, though, it's with HOW we do it.

Dr. Newton's goal was to therapeutically help those who entrusted themselves to his care, enabling them to discover the source, or sources, of thought that disturbed them and impaired their functioning. After initially realizing what he had tapped onto, he also thought to enrich others' lives by allowing them to discover hidden realities of the "larger world" engulfing us all. Dr. Newton in his book *Journey of Souls* indicated that he operated on the premise that no emotional or mental health impairment is imaginary. His goal was to empower his patients so that they could become the most important source of their own well-being through a recognition of the "big picture." His intellectual curiosity and motivations widened, however, when the insights his patients achieved through therapy not only transformed their lives but also greatly impacted his. That led to these two major works, and more beyond them not covered here.

Dr. Newton helped his patients by asking them, through hypnotherapy, to take themselves to the source of their pain. The insights achieved by his patients helped him ask deeper questions about the meaning and purpose of life, questions that are often thought of in our society to be perhaps more of a religious or philosophical nature. However, we as a race are gradually (maybe not so gradually now) discovering that what we thought of as spiritual previously is every bit as much a part of the real, physical world as things we can touch.

There is no doubt that society is today undergoing a radical, foundational change. Because what does it base its moral judgments on? Even politicians like Senator Chris Murphy and others are calling for a "new spirituality" as an anecdote to society's needs today (calling for this in 2023).

Because of science seeping into the mindset of even those who do not know science, we are turned off by religious tenets we suspect not to be true.

When the foundation of society's moral basis of judgment is swept away, everything tends to topple. You can see just that today. Society largely does not trust long-trusted institutions. People, who no longer have a foundational basis for understanding what is right and what is wrong, can get pretty crazy! Many revert to an animal-like adherence to their "tribe" – and reason be damned.

Dr. Newton was a man who came to see this new spirituality his patients presented to him, which he reluctantly accepted, as right in the middle of atheism and Ill-fitting, pious religion. It presented a whole new way of looking at WHAT IS. If it were understood, he believed in his later life that it was just what society needs now.

Dr. Newton also kept away from hypnotically taking his patients into their past lives. He did not initially believe in that either. Only when he was stunned when asking a hypnotized patient to take herself to the "source of her pain," and she went into a past life, did it dawn on him that there might be something to the idea of past lives. His next patient, to whom the same thing happened, turned him around and set his life on his work which will, hopefully and ultimately, change the world again.

Dr. Newton would not say he did anything other than respond to what his patients told him. In other words, the consciousness, which infuses everything with existence, seems to know what we need and when we need it.

May you marvel at these new insights as others, surely including me, have.

~

This book started as a book written by Jim Burch and Jim's friend Nick Brogno together. But after months of writing, it became obvious that they wrote to different audiences: Jim to a more generalist type of audience, and Nick to a more scholarly audience. And Jim concentrated on insights and revelations from the recent discoveries of Dr. Michael Newton, while Nick focused on the traditional philosophical outlook. Also, the book as written together became quite voluminous (imagine a book three or four times this size). So, they decided to pare it down and each to write his book on this topic, with insights from the other and each to their different audience.

That is what this book is: it is written by Jim Burch, but Nick Brogno has occasionally offered insights from his perspective. Usually, you will not know when that has happened. When Jim was writing, Nick's observations were woven in, sometimes writing a sentence or two here and there, sometimes more, but not noted as such. Jim has done that for Nick's book as well. Very rarely you may find the same sentence or two in both of their books.

Nick's book is entitled: ***A Door to Willingness and Trust: Going Beyond Our Circumstances***. The book is like this one in its unique direction on this singular subject. Nick's is more broad and more scholarly than mine. Both express a viewpoint, a different one in fact, that each human being will have his/her own perspective dictated by experiences, heredity, culture, geographic home port, nature, AND nurture. Neither is "correct" to the exclusion of the other, because people are at different points in their lives, their formations, and their jumping-off points.

We hope you will find both books enlightening.

TABLE OF CONTENTS
Foreword 3
Table of Contents 7
Introduction 12

BOOK 1 – The UNIQUE Dr. Michael Newton 21

Chapter 1. **Meet Dr. Newton** 22
Chapter 2. **But Were His Findings Fabricated or Real?** 28

BOOK 2 – The Explosive Discoveries of Dr. Michael Newton 39

Chapter 3. **Powerful Indeed** ... 40
Chapter 4. **Transitioning from Earthy Life to Eternal Life** ... 45

- No Such Thing as Death
- Staying in Contact with the Deceased
- Settling In, on the Other Side
- What Is Your Cluster and What Do You Do There
- Leisure Activities and Physical Love in the Spiritual World
- Council of Elders
- The Presence
- Journey Onward

Chapter 5. **The Growth Process of Souls** ... 74

- The Birth of Souls
- Beginner Souls
- Intermediate Souls
- The Space of Transformation
- Spiritual Learning Centers
- Soul Specializations
- Graduation from the Primary Soul Group
- The Advanced Soul
- Life Selections
- Choosing a New Body
- Preparation for Embarkment/the Place of Recognition
- Rebirth
- Joining of Soul and Body
- Soul Division and Reunification

Chapter 6. **Guides** ... 109
Chapter 7. **Some Characteristics of Universal Life** ... 114

- Soulmates
- Categories of Soulmates
- Hybrid Souls
- Some Souls Can End Their Own Existence
- Transformers
- Souls of Solitude
- Ghosts and Other Souls Who Won't Go On
- Discarnates Who Visit Earth
- Possession
- Walk-ins
- The Levels of Growth
- Auras and Levels of Spiritual Attainment
- The Four General Types of Souls
- The Spirit World
- The Spirit World Is Orderly and Structured

- Memory
- Other "Worlds"
- Timelessness

Chapter 8. **What We Call "Hell" Is Not** 143
Chapter 9. **Questions and Observations** 150

- Do Animals Have Souls?
- Suicide
- Abortion
- Gays and Lesbians and Other Sexual Types
- The Future on Earth
- Other Universes

Chapter 10. **The Source** 160

- Traditional Christian Teaching
- We Want to Become God

Chapter 11. **The Impact of Dr. Newton's New Perspective** ... 168

**BOOK 3 – What All That Means for Us
(Everybody Wants to Go to "Heaven")** 174

Chapter 12. **Highlights from These Discoveries** 175
Chapter 13. **A New Perspective ... Way Beyond Past Understanding** 178

- The Breakthrough
- The Revelation
- Lives on This Planet

- The Purpose of Our Existence
- Our Goal is to Become God

Chapter 14. **What Hypnotic Regressions Tell Us About Fuller Life** 187

- The Other Side, Our Spiritual Home
- Our Beginning
- Incarnations on Earth

Chapter 15. **Living on the Other Side** ... 193

- Back "Home"
- The Displaced Soul
- Our Heavenly Journey
- Settling In, at Home

Chapter 16. **Itches** 202

- The Source of Our Conflicts on Earth
- Again, That Incomprehensible Source
- An Itch for Change: Reborn Again
- Getting Ready to Go Back
- Another Earthly Life!

Chapter 17. **Traditional (Big Time) Misunderstandings/Mistakes** 212

- Carnal Desires (Sex)
- Is There Really Any Such Thing as "Evil"?
- Then What is "Sin"?
- Our Concept of God
- Jesus
- Our "Special Relationship" with God

Chapter 18. **Home!** ... 224

- There is Only One

A Final Thought ... 230
    Biographies ... 231

INTRODUCTION

In the books *Journey of Souls* and *Destiny of Souls* written by Dr. Michael Newton, there is an assumption consistent with what most religious, and many theists, perceive to be true: life here on earth is only one dimension of a larger reality – *we live forever*. Dr. Michael Newton, however, comes from more of a scientific point of view in arriving at his conclusions rather than a religious, theological, or even philosophical position. Dr. Michael Newton, from a psychological or psychiatric perspective, used techniques of hypnosis to tap the unconscious experiences of a large number of people, ultimately totaling more than 7,000 subjects from varied backgrounds. Dr. Newton's books are compilations of subliminal material reported by multiple people while in a hypnotic state, as well as his own interpretation of those findings.

New concepts discussed in this book may not fit individual worldviews, those formed by years of personal and social experience which may include religious beliefs or non-religious determinations derived from religious beliefs. For example, the titles of the two books, *Journey of Souls* and *Destiny of Souls,* might disturb some people given concepts like "soul" or "after-life," especially if one comes from an atheistic perspective. Differing "points of view," as defined through terminology, might be troubling. Some might disregard such concepts, making us unwilling to even entertain them.

Wherever your perspective has you in its grip now, you are going to be surprised (shocked? amazed? dumbfounded? skeptical?) at least several times by what you read in this book. It is so new to us. Some say "refreshing." Some say "shocking." I, myself, couldn't quite believe everything I read on a page, until I turned that page, found something even more revealing, and at the same time then found that I believed the previous page. In other words, this will take some getting used to.

You, the reader, are hereby asked to consider that the concept and practice of science have broadened over the last century or so. No longer do we just consider tangible things as the purview of science. We now count things – ethereal though they may be – that we can count, categorize, and assess because numerous individuals *think* the same thing (psychology), respond the same way to similar stimuli (sociology), leave tell-tale signs behind that cause us to think about what that meant to them (anthropology), etc.

The real, ultimate questions are why are we here? What is our relationship with whatever it is that humanity has termed "Divinity"? What is our relationship with one another? How do we come to know this Divinity, this All-Loving Awareness – if at all – that most people today refer to as "God" (among the monumental number of names given to it), which is beyond all understanding?

There are two monumental occurrences in the modern world. Without them, none of what we write would be presented, would not be a problem, and would not cause us to have to consider it.

The **first** is that we have discovered what past philosophers and, indeed, all thinkers from ages past never knew. They simply *knew* that this physical world was as permanent as anything could ever be – of course it was: you can feel it and see it and breathe it. They never could realize, until modern science discovered it as true, that everything made of atoms (a "new" concept) was itself at its core, always and everywhere. Moreover, atoms are just a projection of ENERGY. We now know – unlike even relatively recent past times – that energy is the movement of consciousness. Consciousness is what we humans have traditionally called "God."

Quite simply, this changes everything for all time. Nothing physical is permanent.

Are we? Our physical bodies are not permanent; they are composed of atoms, and we can see that they return to the elements. But how about that which makes *us*? That is, is this consciousness with which I know myself to be everlasting? Or does it disappear when my body does?

The **second** discovery is history. We can now look back far, very far, into the past and see trends, see patterns, see when – with the benefit of hindsight – there appear to have been great leaps of understanding within humanity. Why did these occur? Why did leaps of consciousness, of bright new understandings, crash land into humanity and then spread like wildfire?

This leads again and ultimately to that eternal question: Why did I come here? For what purpose did I come here?

The truth is that we all come here to BE challenged, to see to what extent we can change our minds, broaden our perspective, see new realities, and be open to the world and to God/Divinity/Loving Consciousness/All-Loving Awareness or whatever name you choose to call this mystery of everything that presents itself to us here, as presented to us in the world. Nothing surprising there; it is the reason for this world's existence. We need CHALLENGES so that our life forces, or what others might call our souls, can develop and grow. This is the place. We will always have challenges here; we need to face them if we are to grow and develop emotionally and/or spiritually.

Change produces challenges. Yet, that is exactly what many individuals of all ages fight: change. They are uncomfortable when something changes.

Today, we have a system of beliefs that have been commonly held since before the Middle Ages. Through Dr. Newton's use of a relatively new science in hypnosis, a whole new interpretation of human experience is achieved. Dr. Newton assisted people in retrieving unconsciously but purposefully forgotten or repressed memories. Most people DO purposefully forget past life experiences because it is a lot of baggage to carry around when our primary task is to be attentive to the soul-changing opportunities of experience in THIS life.

Dr. Newton and his students have indeed met many subjects who had come to see him because of troubles in their lives. But many others came to see him because they were simply interested in their greater purpose in life. So, not all were troubled. Nevertheless, it is worth noting that if the purpose of this life is to experience challenges to grow and challenges are also known as problems, then most of us lead a normal, somewhat-troubled life mixed in with the beauty within this universe.

Dr. Newton's contribution, side-by-side with traditional interpretive frameworks, proposes that we might look at the world, and our place in it, from a completely different perspective. We can choose to look at it from a perspective of how we think about other matters where we are comfortable, or we might try a completely different perspective by challenging long-honed and ingrained understandings. This is very thought-provoking but emotionally difficult. This "new" introduction to human society, which challenges our belief systems, is not entirely unheralded in that it has happened before, as times often dictate the need to change perspectives. The need to change gives us an opportunity for us to alter our Self-Consciousness, leading to a new level of awareness about the world in which we live, and our place within it.

While acknowledging that every time and every period is filled with the challenges of change, there do come times in the rolling of history when humanity has accelerated the solutions to the changes of earlier times and is ready to confront new challenges. That is when the guiding hand of the conscious universe injects another realization into our midst. It's always "scientific," always "natural." Although, it may not seem scientific or natural at the time. Such a major injection into the human perspective is looking at humanity's origin, place, and destiny from a completely new perspective and new framework. It's the result of Dr. Michael Newton's poking and prodding of the unconscious until he found a new layer of life underneath what we already knew. In doing that, he broadened immensely our understanding of the panorama of life. This interjection of a new level of consciousness is not new in the history of humanity.

Dr. Newton himself would be the first to tell you that he did nothing special. But those of us from the outside who look at what he did beg to differ. He was a most uncommonly talented man, a man of brilliant training, of a very pleasant character, and with an ability to think things through to their logical conclusions without leading questions. He faced answers to the questions that come up undauntingly, without fear of where they might take him (and us), determined to present "what is."

As we look back on the long slough of history, we can see that consciousness has broken through into humanity in giant awakenings not at all through our own devices, because they always surprise us. What came to Dr. Newton – against his will and his inclinations, beliefs, and proclivities – was just that: consciousness using him as the right vehicle.

Through an innovative "spiritual perspective" beyond material reality alone, the element and substance of what was always commonly meant as "God" intervening dramatically and radically into history might be better understood as opportunities for change and periods of metanoia. Actually, "intervening ... into history" is not quite the right description in that Divinity is the SOURCE of history and all physical reality, and history and human reality exist WITHIN Divinity.

These opportunities to change bring us to new levels of awareness. This is not only so that we can adapt to an emerging new world, where transformation occurs through moments of decision, but also so that we can use what we have before us NOW to grow our souls, not some antiquated viewpoint that no longer quite fits the bill. These moments of decision, from a spiritual perspective, could be viewed as a reincarnation by some or perhaps even as an ongoing incarnation by others. As those explaining reincarnation to those not believing in it often say, "Is it any more unbelievable that we should be born many times than that we should be born once?"

These moments for a decision can also be considered as a recapitulation of what happened initially in creation as understood from diverse religious points of view. It might also be viewed by some as "individuated souls," emerging from within a Conscious Energy State. This from a traditional perspective might be labeled as God that precedes matter. Others from a metaphysical perspective might just label it as being, existence, origin, or beginning while others might call it the "Big Bang," as it has become known in science, not at all personal, and without any type of ultimate meaning and purpose. It is from a person's point of view, otherwise known as a religious or "belief" perspective, that it or existence becomes infused with meaning and purpose. In which case, it might be conceived as Conscious Energy, God-incarnated which first entered primates and other sentient life forms hundreds of thousands of years ago. Perhaps at other times, it might be much earlier than that, and perhaps often.

Divine Consciousness, or God erupting into human lives yet again, might also be perceived as what happens when humanity moves from a collective concept of self, in which living under the dictates of God and King/State was sufficiently rewarding, to no longer being so, moving humanity to a new level of awareness to become champions of concepts like individual human dignity and liberty. This kind of phenomenon could have also gone on unnoticed any number of other times, all leading to different levels of awareness, periods of enlightenment, and new points of view.

While it is true that society has traditionally throughout its history changed only gradually in a long-term ongoing process, sometimes expressed by an old axiom, "God writes straight with crooked lines," Dr. Newton's work and that of his successors have introduced a different framework into the societal picture. They suggest we may need to look at the world and our place in it from a completely distinctive perspective.

Like individual lives, the history of human society looks like this: extremely slow ("plenty of time!") as we look forward, but as we look to the past, extremely fast like a rocket ship (Ask any older person.).

Journey of Souls and *Destiny of Souls* create several questions about life, what we know, and consciousness, but it also gives new answers and new insights to many questions that were beginning to pile up from the limited and rather non-expansive religious thinking of centuries past. Most of us have likely thought about what it means to be conscious. And because of this, at some point or other, we have compared ourselves with other living beings and have observed differences. It is likely many of us see ourselves as superior in the hierarchy of species, and – since Aristotle – define ourselves in like manner as "rational animals," giving us a distinction from microscopic life, other mammals, birds, fish, and amphibians. Many, given the insights of Darwin and the survival of the species and/or from long-held religious beliefs, see humankind as the pinnacle of evolution. And it certainly is (... but only as far as we know!)

Most of us probably don't even question what we know and how we know it, or even think about our place in the universe. Why are we here? Some of us may not even think about whether or not we have any ultimate purpose or think about our purpose and the meaning of our life. The accumulation of material things, the size of a portfolio, our comparisons to one another, and survival are often the only things many might think about. That is certainly okay, in that THAT is the PURPOSE of our being here to experience those kinds of life encounters. But there is a whole lot more going on within us as we experience such activities. As we go through this life, we decidedly achieve the experiences we come here for, and we prepare ourselves for emerging challenges to come either in this life or in others. That is why, regretfully, we can live the longest life known and will have to admit at the end that we are not "done" yet.

Life with its immediate pleasures and pains is enough at the moment until confronted with our finiteness, causing us to question more deeply. Is there a reason for our existence, or is it just by chance that we are here? This question about purpose usually confronts most of us as we grow older and more immediately face our mortality. Or perhaps we may ask such questions in situations when we experience the death of someone we love or through a tragic experience. Thus, the seasons of life.

Thus, death and the passage of one life would be a lot easier to take if we realized that we have moved quite slowly toward a goal of perfection. We do not have to *complete* the work in this single lifetime. *We have all the time in the world.* We will be back, once rested, to take up new challenges.

But if each life is but a steppingstone, what is our real life like? What is it like where we have our permanent home? What do we do when we are there? Will I like it?!?!

Here, I will attempt to explore the work of Dr. Newton, how it relates to questions of consciousness and ultimate meaning, and how it compares to philosophies of the past. Because the concepts of morality and how things exist have been ingrained within us since the birth of most humans since the Middle Ages, we are likely to assume those beliefs even without thinking of them. The concepts provided through the work of Dr. Michael Newton, however, are quite new in history and you are probably not familiar with them ... yet. Therefore, we start with an introduction to Dr. Newton's earthquake of consciousness-enlightenment.

Please note that, as I mentioned elsewhere but want to make certain that you don't miss this point, there are portions of this book that

are taken verbatim from Dr. Newton's books even though I could no longer identify the portions that are lifted.

This all happened because when I first made a 62-page series of "notes" from *Journey of Souls* and *Destiny of Souls* for my benefit and study, I had no idea that I would ever use them in a published book. So, I took some of those notes verbatim, not referencing them.

You will find many of my ideas mixed in with Dr. Newton's. Please don't blame him if you find my ideas not quite as satisfying as his! *To me*, however, they complement Dr. Newton's works and make them more understandable. I will say it again, with emphasis: to get the full impact and the clearest picture of Dr. Newton's monumentally important work, work that thrusts humanity almost light years ahead of where it was, you should read the books themselves. Don't miss the full beauty of these books.

BOOK 1
The UNIQUE Dr. Michael Newton (1931-2016)

Chapter 1
Meet Dr. Newton

Dr. Michael Newton (1931-2016) in his introduction to his first book *Journey of Souls* tells us something about himself. He was a professional and a scholar, who made it his life's work to help people who had been suffering psychologically, losing a sense of meaning and purpose in their lives, and perhaps losing even self-identity which ultimately led them to him. This would have been very consistent with why a therapist might wish to use regressive hypnosis. Probably, many of Dr. Newton's clients had experienced some type of trauma. This refers in the largest measure to Dr. Newton's early subjects, and psychological trauma was not necessarily quite as prevalent in his later subjects' current lives as it was in his earlier subjects.

He also described himself as a specialist in behavior modification for the treatment of psychological disorders. Dr. Newton best seemed to describe his beliefs about therapy as a relationship with his clients, stating, "Together, we elicit the meaning, function, and consequences of their beliefs because I take the premise that no mental problem is imaginary."

Dr. Newton in his introduction also described himself as a "skeptic by nature," who may have had a sense of intellectual curiosity about such things as, for example, belief systems or anything of a spiritual nature some might have expressed to have given them meaning and purpose. He did not describe himself as a religious or spiritual advisor in any manner.

In Dr. Newton's introduction, he also revealed his awareness of criticism from within the field of psychology and psychiatry regarding the use of regressive hypnosis. He was fully aware of critics who suggest that the hypnotic suggestion used to induce an unconscious state might itself be a source for fabricated memories. However, he believed that his clients really took the lead, and his method of inquiry was for them to disclose what they interpreted as possible factors to the emotional disturbance that led them to seek help in the first place.

He thought that through his method of critical inquiry, he was able to distinguish the hypnotic "experiences" of his clients from any confabulations they may have mentally constructed. Through cross-examination and a phenomenological record of each case, Dr. Newton found no evidence of anyone, intentionally or unintentionally, distorting a spiritual experience from within a hypnotic state. As attested by his introduction, he was fully convinced about the truthfulness of the experiences communicated by his subjects in a hypnotic state. He further perceived himself as having been fully able to distinguish the memories of his subjects while under hypnosis from any of their known histories and/or religious belief systems.

In expressing how his subjects may have impacted him, Dr. Netwon reported the case of one subject who most emotionally moved him from a state of curious interest to a state of fascination when her emotional pain was one of a deep sense of loneliness. This one subject found it extremely hard to become comfortable and content in the state of hypnosis. Upon inquiry, while being in the hypnotic state, the woman blurted out, "I miss some friends in my group and that's why I get so lonely on earth." Through further questioning, she thought of her permanent home not being Earth but being with her friends in another realm, whom she said she was looking at while in the hypnotic state. Dr. Newton recognized that this woman's experience revealed a spirit world that involved an extension of past life regression, and she longed for her "friends" not of this earth.

Dr. Newton indicated that he thought of consciousness as three concentric circles, each smaller than the last and within the other, separated by layers of mind-consciousness. The outer layer, or the first one, is one that Dr. Newton visualized as the conscious mind, which is one of critical or analytical thinking. He thought of this outer layer of consciousness to be most connected with our physical bodies and physical experience. The second concentric circle perceived by Dr. Newton is within the first and is the consciousness he thought of as being our memories, what can also be called the subconscious, or what others might think of as implied and explicit memories from our experiences in the physical world, former lives, and current life. The third concentric circle within the first and second concentric circles is what he called the superconscious mind, which is the Self as an expression of a higher power.

The superconscious mind, as Dr. Newton defined it, represents our highest center of wisdom and perspective. All the information about life after death comes from this source of intelligent energy. The superconscious mind is our truest identity. It's the "soul" as Dr. Newton called it, which he accepted a priori as containing all alter-egos or personalities we may have ever taken on within our life or lifetimes. De. Newton may not have said it, but I believe it is also within – connected, part of, an individuated manifestation of – the All of It, which we call God, Allah, Higher Consciousness, All- Loving Awareness, or any number of names.

In the sleep state, Dr. Newton perceived that messages from the brain are dropped into the subconscious and are vented through dreams, which he thought were not reliable. He conjectured that the accuracy of information gained through hypnotic regression was based on the depth of consciousness tapped. In a state of hypnosis, one in which a person is not dreaming or hallucinating but is in an in-between state that isn't a sleep state or awake state, the subconscious was therefore most reliable.

He reported that the intention of his work was not about reincarnation or past lives and the re-embodiment of souls. It's to capture the subconscious memories of multiple clients in their quest for emotional relief as they attempt to make sense of their life experiences. Dr. Newton suggested that his understanding grew out of the experiences put into language by his clients. He was quite aware that some who read his book might be very skeptical and be unable to accept in any way the concepts expressed in language that is at all spiritual and deny that such ideas could have any existence at all.

Dr. Newton's techniques for hypnotic regression to Life Between Lives have been replicated. The Newton Institute, named after Dr. Michael Newton, trains practitioners – now in their hundreds – to do what Dr. Newton did. Because this is not an exact science yet, some practitioners are better than others. The institute will probably learn to apply more guidelines and endorsements to practitioners who can then be separated – wheat from chaff.

Dr. Newton throws light on the parade of what we think to be true at any one time. In his books, he says over and over again that what we think to be true today may be only an inkling of what we will know to be true tomorrow, and that is only an inkling of what is beyond that. His technique is being put into practice today in the hundreds of hypnotic regressionists being trained and organized at the Newton Institute formed to promulgate his findings and to go beyond them.

Yes, we can see in Dr. Newton's writings how difficult it is to express truly non-physical conditions in the limitation of words and within the limited dimensions we have on this earth. Sometimes, it causes his subjects (who are hypnotized) to laugh out loud!

I believe we are getting closer – and perhaps are already there – to being able to prove things like the existence of an All-Loving Awareness that holds within itself all that is, but not in the kind of "proof" we have previously accepted.

For example, many do not believe in the afterlife because there is no "proof" of it. But neither is there any proof for any of the things that we could describe as what makes each of us so uniquely ourselves. Why do we love this person and not someone else? Why do we get absorbed in and thrive in a certain kind of work ... work others would find quite boring? Why do we enjoy certain hobbies or pastimes that others reject out of hand as not fulfilling? Why do we value truth over lies, or love over fear and hatred? None of those things can be proven. Yet they are the stuff that makes each of us "US."

Chapter 2
But Were His Findings Fabricated or Real?

But were those resurrected memories real or were they fabricated?

Studies indicate that many hypnotic regression memories MAY BE unwittingly fabricated, but critics cannot prove that they are. We just cannot prove it today with today's acceptable measuring standards. Perhaps someday we will be able to, perhaps not. But to think that 7,000 subjects (yes, 7,000!) would be able to fabricate basically the same stories independently of each other would be testing the human brain for susceptibility beyond reason.

Memories of all individuals are notoriously corrupted, bent to answer the individual's problems of today, not when the memories originated. In court trials, for example, it is fairly easy to discount memories of first-hand observations as being inaccurate. The "gist" of most memories may be somewhat close to what happened, but much more often the lesson to be learned from a memory is unintentionally bent to answer *today's* problem by the person who remembers.

However, memories are generally awakened recollections of something that happened previously in this life. A memory drawn from hypnotic regression about circumstances in another type of life may be altogether a different matter. Every subject of hypnotic regression to Life Between Lives is tapping into a level of "memory" not often utilized in this physical life. Moreover, these memories of Life Between Lives bring an understanding and an ability to cope with life anew for most subjects, as opposed to confusion and depression possible from memories from this life.

Thoroughly professional critiques of Dr. Newton's work by renowned investigators of Near-Death Experiences, who themselves had come to believe in Near-Death Experiences but had no experience in Life Between Lives (so new is it to our understanding), failed to mention that Dr. Newton tried assiduously not to lead his subjects. He would say, "What happened before that?" or "Go to an earlier time." They are generalized rather than specific questions. Dr. Newton's subjects went through four to four-and-a-half-hour sessions for just the purpose of eliminating the problems these critics express, rather than one or two-hour sessions.

Dr. Newton's subjects seemed to be different people from what they are in "this life," when under his lengthy hypnotic regression. They are more relaxed, happy to be back "home" on the other side, free of the problems of this life, and generally understanding those problems from the perspective of the other side. When released from hypnotherapy, subjects reverted to the people they had been with the same problems as when they went under hypnosis. But they now had a new understanding of both their purpose in life and of a path toward correction. They often seemed almost refreshed, ready, and eager to experience this life again with more vigor and determination. Such results as these would counter an argument of them getting false memories from misunderstood experiences.

There are a couple of hundred hypnotic regressionists taking subjects through lengthy Life Between Lives encounters, in the way Dr. Newton did, now several years after his death. I do know of one young woman, however, who went to one of the hypnotic regression doctors from the Newton Institute whose advice, as conveyed by the subject, did not seem to be accurate. Whether this was the fault of the subject or the doctor is difficult to know.

There is optimism and hopefulness in this quest for a spirituality that can work in our day and age, giving meaning and purpose to more people.

The work of Dr. Newton has started what now seems so essential to so many. It was science that introduced into society what exactly was the origin and destiny of life – consciousness ("God," if you will) – as determined and announced to the world by chemists in the 19th century. Thereafter, we were introduced into the realm of new acceptable studies, that of consciousness and relativity. Doesn't Einstein's Theory of Relativity – accepted as a theory but also as close to fact as science can get – require that consciousness be at the core of the physical?

Science insists that every human action and reaction (which is everything we humans do, think, and are) is preceded by a fraction of a second biological or chemical inducement in the body. That does not preclude, however, that the soul in its preparation for this life and long before we ever got here could have arranged for those biological or chemical inducements. That does not preclude the possibility that our soul may call upon them before our body even knows.

Do you see what we mean when we say that we have *just begun* to unravel the mystery of our journeys on Earth?

But some can argue for "the old way" too much sometimes.

We are in giant turmoil now. Old solutions and old perspectives don't seem to work for most people. We argue for the old ways because it seemed to work so well in the past (did it?). As such, we therefore think it needs to be imposed on everyone as God's Will until everyone is oriented to one way of thinking. Alternatively, will we be open to new understandings and attempt to unravel old traditions so that we can in some small way come to know this Divinity which is Loving Consciousness, which is truly infinite, beyond all understanding, and is pervasive in everything that is? Will we dialogue with one another, and take in challenges such as those introduced to us in the *Journey of Souls* and *Destiny of Souls* from the studies of Dr. Michael Newton, or just stay where we are?

Only a few of Dr. Newton's subjects had known one another or had been able to compare their backgrounds and beliefs with one another before being placed in a regressive hypnotic state. No leading questions were asked to prompt a response in one direction or another. This gives credence to Dr. Newton's methodology and his findings. Further, whether or not one believes in life after death was not the point of Dr. Newton's study. Rather, Dr. Newton's methodology was to record facts reported by hypnotized individuals. His works are an amazing account rendered by thousands of subjects that fit together as an account of Life Between Lives.

Whether or not the subject was religious or not and whether or not they might have believed in Jesus, Moses, Mohammed, Buddha, or any number of other Masters, not one of them reported meeting or seeing that Master on the other side. None reported a refutation or enlightenment in the dogma of a particular belief. None said, "Ah hah! That other guy was right!" This leads me to believe that all of these Masters were what their adherents believed them to be, and they also were not. They each presented legitimate pathways to the same goal – union with Ultimate All-Loving Awareness achieved by different means depending on where those individuals were in time, place, and earlier experiences.

Dr. Newton simply observed facts as reported by his subjects as he advanced his "Life Between Lives" technique over the decades. And it gradually gathered support and understanding over time. He later founded an institute to carry on, train other practitioners, and further his work. After several years, the foundation's board of directors changed its name to the Newton Institute to honor Dr. Michael Newton's groundbreaking work in founding this field.

Dr. Newton's work is a descriptive methodology, a verbatim recording of intersubjective experiences. The method was more scientific and included sociology and psychology. Therefore, it was unlike the previous conceptual framework that came to us directly from the Middle Ages.

This "science" is the recordation of the personal experiences of people. Dr. Newton then compared their convictions and observations. His evaluation of the concepts of science now includes sociology and psychology. His work comes from no religious/spiritual bias. The beliefs or disbeliefs of Dr. Newton's subjects play no role in their participation in the study. EVERY subject Dr. Newton ever had came back no longer as a "believer" – whether they originally were or not –

but as a **knower** of this Loving Consciousness we call God. Many of those subjects though, when they first came to Dr. Newton for counsel, were once traditional Christians.

First, there is ONLY Loving Consciousness. This Consciousness *moves*. Without movement, consciousness does not exist. In religious language, the movement of consciousness is called "spirit," and Jesus said that the spirit was so powerful that it was "holy." That is the "Holy Spirit" or the movement of this Loving Consciousness in the non-material realm.

Fortunately, Loving Consciousness has provided a place for us, a place where we can grow more quickly than in most other environments: this planet Earth.

The movement of consciousness in scientific language is called energy. The words "energy" and "spirit" only emphasize different aspects of exactly the same thing. Energy vibrates in various times and patterns and forms the 118 atoms in the periodic table. Science 101 tells us that matter (that which is made of atoms) is only energy vibrating at different pulsations. These atoms – of which everything physical is composed – are merely energy manifesting itself as matter. All matter is, at its heart, energy.

As such, everything – EVERYTHING – is an individuated manifestation of that Loving Consciousness, that All-Loving Awareness that we call God, or Allah, or Yahweh, Higher Consciousness, the Divine, Great Spirit, the Force, or any of those hundreds of words we humans use to describe that which is the source and the end of all that is.

In fact, Dr. Newton's studies do not "give great credence to theories or beliefs about reincarnation." Rather, they observe and recount the telling of these apparent facts – "facts" to the experiencers – of thousands of independent subjects.

Our current societal moral foundation is still based on a Medieval outlook. While the Medieval times gave meaning and purpose to people then, it was not life-sustaining, and the overlaying concepts – not the underlying eternal truths – that came from Catholic/Christian thinking then no longer give purpose to people today. Their emphasis on community, a predominant view of the world at the time, indeed was a "life force." It gave meaning and purpose to multitudes of people, but it was not self-sustaining and could not go on forever into the future. The community gave a sense of security and trust about what was real and what was false, grounded in the beliefs of Catholicism. There was no separation between Church and State, the Secular and the Profane.

"Catholic" perspective (i.e., "universal" ... i.e., it doesn't work if it doesn't bring in everybody of all faiths and geographic regions because it would not be "universal") is much deeper in Dr. Newton's conclusions than that shallow understanding of calcified thoughts from the Middle Ages. Building on it from understandings of science applied to spiritual reality, EVERYTHING is an expression, a unique manifestation of that consciousness we call "God." Science tells us that consciousness is the source and the destiny of everything physical. Our life force, our "soul" originates within this consciousness – before it ever manifests itself here as things made of matter – and is therefore perfect, but not yet perfectly formed. We come here for the challenges (AKA, "problems") by which we accelerate the growth process of our souls. We experiment. And through that, we come to understand not only who we ARE, but also who we ARE NOT. This is so that we can then more passionately become who we are.

That is the logical and most profound understanding of where we come to that we ultimately can infer from Dr. Newton's work. It draws in other knowledge that science points toward today.

Dr. Newton could not have created, together with over 7,000 other individuals, such a coherent set of perceptions as laid out in his books. I don't know who would have wanted to devote a lifetime to such a subterfuge, especially when you observe Dr. Newton in his videos on YouTube. Clearly, this is not a man prone to subterfuge.

I also do not believe that any individual has to jettison the traditions that have made him who he is. For example, I am also a product of a Catholic upbringing. I have found that while I no longer believe those disciplinary Catholic tenets in the same manner I once did, I have come to understand their deeper meanings and connotations. I have built UPON them, not jettisoned them. Others are doing the same.

Regarding the loss of traditions, Dr. Newton's works are true. Your latest (in this life) traditions did not make you who you are. Your experiences and resultant memories (mistakes and lessons learned) from your long journey (but short because eternity is the longest experience) allowed YOU to create who you are from WITHIN the Loving Consciousness that is All of It. Each of life's experiences created who you were in that lifetime, but the cascading memories of experiences of many lifetimes (and perhaps much more, many other types of experiences yet unknown) "created" your soul and your "self" as it exists in your Life Between Lives. It's your permanent abode when material things are gone.

The material world neither permanently enslaves us nor permanently prevents us from being who we truly are. It is, rather, our tool for soul growth. The material world presents us with challenges and opportunities that result in our soul's growth so that we may BECOME who we truly can be.

When you look back at all those Medieval thinkers who set the tone for us today, they seem so elementary. And they were. Humanity was elementary. We know infinitely more now. And yet, millennia from now, WE seem to be so elementary in our thinking. And souls of that time will be aware of so much more that we do not know presently. Consciousness will continue to intrude.

This reality of Life Between Lives is not a progression of ideas transformed into language and recognized in the flow of history. It is, rather, an observation and recitation of Consciousness injecting itself through one of its most impulsive expansions into the history of humanity. It is an observation of new understandings, heretofore relatively unknown, breaking forth in new human techniques (hypnotic regressions) and revealing new (formerly buried) truths in new ways. There's nothing new, but some things are learned for the first time in human history.

Within the historic parade of enlightenment over the centuries, Dr. Newton brings to light new expressions of truth, heretofore only guessed at. That is what is important.

What does Life Between Lives mean for each of us as an individual and collectively as a society? It is going to have a major impact if enough people absorb the reality of its import.

And history tells us that enough people will indeed absorb it. CHANGE in society does not come about when 50% of the people believe something new, not even 25%. Change begins to happen in a society when 4% of the population believes something new! That is the reason things seem to change so fast.

An individual – troubled or not at one time or another – can realize that his/her life force (soul) is PERFECT. It is here for a purpose devised by itself for his or her growth and knows that experiencing this reality in all its glory and all its doom is the way to greater freedom, insight, and soul development. With that knowledge, it changes EVERYTHING for that individual and makes his/her acceptance of circumstances so much better understood and lived.

The main importance of Newton's revelations regarding the source and the destination of each human life is that it answers conditions that have heretofore been unanswerable. Why do I have problems in my life? How could I be the object of so much bad luck and misery? Do I just have to take it on faith that I live forever? Why can't I just get myself straightened out and stay happy for the rest of my life instead of new problems coming one after the other?

Those answers to old questions ("Problems are how you grow;" "The more problems you face in life, the faster you accelerate spiritually;" "Now you know the purpose of your life is to grow through challenges while enjoying earth's beauty and the friendships of other humans;" "You have selected all the challenges you have, and no one else.") unalterably change one's outlook on existence itself. They make *all the difference in the world.*

The eye-openers in the books about Life Between Lives do not contradict – in any major way – the basic, underlying tenants of any major religious thought. These revelations, for example, did not push the author's own belief in the substance of true (real) Christianity. Rather, they were built on top of that substance. They filled in the holes, made the ridiculous things seem insignificant, created new pathways of understanding, and gave optimism to life. There is no evidence that Dr. Newton's subjects were turned off, angry, or rejecting past BASIC belief systems.

The understanding of Life Between Lives will form a new basis of acceptance and agreement among all kinds of believers.

Dr. Newton introduces a new reality: reports of Life Between Lives previously unheard of and not possible to have been conceived.

In an email to this author, Dr. Newton not long before his death stated that he had over 7,000 subjects, only a few of which are referenced in these books. You will not get the kind of logical support you may wish or need by reading this summary, as you would if you read the books themselves even though much of it is word-for-word to merge the two books of Dr. Newton.

You should also note, as mentioned several times in this book so that you won't miss it, that these selections from Dr. Newton's books are mine alone and are arranged by me. They probably do not reflect what another person doing a summary would select or what Dr. Newton would have selected. Moreover, some parts of this summary are direct quotes without quotation marks. This happened because when I first synthesized this book, I did not know it was going into a book. It was for my use only. Now I have to admit to some copying, but I acknowledge it and honor Dr. Newton through it. Any incoherent thoughts, however, are entirely mine.

BOOK 2
The Explosive Discoveries of Michael Newton, PhD:

A synthesis and arrangement in summary form of
Journey of Souls and Destiny of Souls by Michael Newton, PhD

Note: This is a summary by Jim Burch. It is not done by Dr. Newton or the Newton Institute, who undoubtedly would have arranged it differently and with different emphasis. It shows how Dr. Newton's revelations have impacted one man (me) and highlights what appeared to be important to me. To get the full perspective of the beauty of Dr. Newton's work, please read the books Journey of Souls *and* Destiny of Souls.

(Please remember as you read this book that we are using human words and concepts to describe something in a completely different experience that cannot be described in human words.)

Chapter 3
Powerful Indeed

It did not matter if a person was an atheist, deeply religious, or believed in any philosophical persuasion in between. Once they were in the proper superconscious state of hypnosis, all subjects were consistent in their reports.

Journey of Souls was a pilgrimage through the spirit world on the great river of eternity.

Destiny of Souls is intended to convey travelers on a second expedition along the river with side trips up major tributaries for mere detailed explorations. It's to expand our understanding of the incredible sense of order and planning that exists for the benefit of human beings.

They are merged here in this synopsis, which constitutes Chapter 3.

The term "soul" is used here. That is meant as an individuated piece of universal Consciousness (a Loving Consciousness) that is usually referred to as God, Allah, Jehovah, Yahweh, Higher Consciousness, Higher Power, Divinity, Great Spirit, The Force, and the hundreds of other human language words used to convey that which gives life and existence to all that is. That individuated piece of Loving Consciousness we call a soul is formed within that Consciousness, not outside of it (nothing is outside of it). That individuated spark of existence lasts beyond the body it bonds with. It is eternal because its source is eternal.

Albert Einstein once wrote: "We are slowed down sound and light waves, a walking bundle of frequencies tuned into the cosmos. We are souls dressed up in sacred biochemical garments and our bodies are the instruments through which our souls play their music."

Dr. Newton writes: "*The soul has such majesty that it is beyond description.* I tend to think of souls as intelligent light forms of energy." And "this energy appears to function as vibrational waves similar to electromagnetic force, but without the limitations of charged particles of matter. Soul energy does not appear to be uniform. Like a fingerprint, each soul has a unique identity in its formation, composition, and vibrational distributions."

If the soul's existence begins and is molded by pure thought, it is sustained by that thought as an immortal being. The soul's individual character enables it to influence its physical environment to give greater harmony and balance to life. Souls are an expression of beauty, imagination, and creativity.

The importance of an awareness of our real inner Self cannot be overemphasized for a productive life.

Every soul has a distinctive mental vibrational pattern like a fingerprint. The pattern is similar to a tightly woven basket with interlocking energy strands surrounding an individual core of character. The strands are motion pictures of thought where transference is voluntary to the soul. These involve ideas, concepts, meanings, symbols, and personal distinctions particular to the soul. With experience, during Level III or later (we will address levels later), the soul has the ability within this telepathic world to create any picture frame at any moment. Thus, while nothing is hidden in a general way, no strand opens to the core to release a fine distinction of thought unless a soul wishes another to enter.

Most people who go through a hypnotic regression to Life Between Lives talk of an *indescribable sense of joy and freedom from learning their true identity.*

Most people who hold very traditional religious views seem the most afraid of death. In the last third of the 20th Century in the U.S., it was estimated that 40% of America's citizens believed in reincarnation. This change in attitude has made acceptance of death a little easier for those people who have become more spiritual and are pulling away from a belief in oblivion after life.

We can question whether our universe is all an illusion. If eternal thoughts of the soul are represented by intelligent light energy that is timeless and formless, it is not restricted by matter in our universe. Thus, if a cosmic consciousness controls what the observer mind sees on earth, the whole concept of cause and effect within given time intervals is a manipulated illusion designed to train us. Even if we believe that everything we think is real is really an illusion, life is anything but meaningless. We know if we hold a rock in our hand that it is as real to us as an observer-participant in a physical world. We must also keep in mind that a divine intelligence places us in this environment to learn and grow for the greater good. None of us are here by accident and neither are those events that affect us in our reality at this moment in time.

As you read on regarding your real home, your Life Between Lives, you will feel aware and recognize it, at least to some degree. It will gradually come back to you that, as strange as this mode of living may be to us now, it is true and it is real. You will remember. You will also feel, at the same time, that this is the strangest thing you have ever heard, that it is far from anything you have ever experienced and could ever experience all at the same time.

We now live in a partial world, a world of experience unlike any other, all so that we can change *our* minds about how things are and how they should be. We can now understand who we truly are through experiences. It's on purpose that we only experience part of who we truly are here. We choose to do so with enthusiasm from the other side.

You will probably think at least once, "Who made this stuff up?" It can sound pretty outlandish at first ... until it settles in.

One thing to remember is that this is the compilation of 7,000 or so hypnotic regressions where none of those who regressed were told what the others had said. They all started fresh, and they all ended up complimenting the others' perspectives.

Moreover, Dr. Newton did not ask leading questions. He asked open-ended questions. "Where are you?" rather than "Are you in another life?" They're all intended to not prejudice the hypnotized person.

This is as close to objectivity as one can get.

Chapter 4
Transitioning from Earthly Life to Eternal Life

Reincarnation

Only reincarnation and the concept of the soul have any validity, not because Dr. Newton says so but because his studies show no other option. But "validity" is not the right word, "recounted importance" would do better. Moreover, as previously mentioned, not even one of those subjects ever recounted seeing Jesus, Buddha, Moses, or any of the other human Masters who have so influenced human history at their death when many traditional religionists look forward to "seeing _____" (fill in the blank with the name of the spiritual founder) when they die. That anticipation about seeing the leader of their religion appears to be man-made, perhaps to help them understand their timely circumstances. Those are the conclusions of thousands of studies, and not even one of those studies gave the importance to these subjects' main historical affiliation – Jesus, salvation, sin, etc. – that Christianity does. Most of us in America come from a tradition where Jesus was indeed at the heart of human purpose. His powerful life, teachings, and deeds are brought forth differently in new language and concepts by Dr. Newton through thousands of voices. Jesus himself was not interested in establishing a religion where he would be worshiped. Rather, he was immensely interested in telling others how to find joy and purpose in THEIR lives, and how to transform their individual lives.

Let's look at what a "soul" is based on Newton's findings (not "from" Newton's findings, but rather "based upon" those findings and more from relatively recent scientific revelations).

ONLY (Loving) Consciousness exists ... anywhere. As noted previously this Consciousness *moves*, and does not exist absent it. The movement of consciousness, from one point of view, is called "spirit," and Jesus said that the spirit was so powerful that it was "holy." That is the "Holy Spirit." It's the movement of this Loving Consciousness in the non-material realm. This is the "All-Loving Awareness," the "Loving Consciousness" that has existed eternally long before this consciousness has been manifesting itself as the energy that underlies all things physical.

That original consciousness is constantly moving. Think of fog that is light instead of vapor. When it bunches together in certain densities, it sometimes achieves a self-realization. That self-realization is one of our souls. We are all formed in this way. Nothing new, just a rearrangement of what was. God looks at us as perfect, just not fully formed yet. All-Loving Awareness wants to help us to grow! And so as we look around at this perfect environment in which we find ourselves, we now want to grow and advance to become what is our potential. We look for a place to advance the quickest. We look for someplace with challenges, because challenges are how we grow through the overcoming of obstacles. Where we originate has no obstacles, it is also perfect.

Fortunately, Loving Consciousness has provided at least one place for us, probably many more, this planet Earth.

The movement of consciousness, from another point of view, is called energy. Atoms, which compose everything physical, are merely energy manifesting itself AS matter. At its heart, all matter is energy. And energy is the movement of consciousness.

As such, everything is an individuated manifestation of that Loving Consciousness that we call God. Science confirms the basis of all religions.

The Medieval perspective does not at all express the viewpoint of Jesus. When we have dug to the depths of the meaning of Jesus' teachings, buried so long in understandings of the times 2,000 years ago, we come to conclude that the evil we do here is evil only so long as we will not have yet concluded that we have tried those things and they are not working for us at all. The moment we conclude that we must choose a new path, the better path objectively, those past "sins" become "blessings" because they will have taught us who we are so that we can more passionately pursue who we truly are. That is the very purpose of life, as one that is allowed to blossom by this All-Loving Awareness.

Medieval philosophies fished around for justice and an explanation for life and its circumstances. *Journey of Souls* is a recitation of individuals who speak with certainty about what they have experienced. Dr. Newton puts it all together.

The medieval perspective reflects the "religion" that the teachings of Christ had morphed into a cut-and-dry adhesion to "teachings" and to what one was allowed to do and not to do. Thanks to modern telecommunications and technology, we have been able to gather up the fragments of early biblical texts (an extraordinary few exist from the earliest centuries) and compare them using computers with what we have today and what we have postulated as rigidly true ... and we have found them substantially lacking.

We also know Jesus spoke in the Aramaic language, not the Greek the Gospels were written in so that they could be passed around the known civilized world. And that Aramaic was a dramatically different language from Greek. In Greek, "this word" could mean one or two things. But in the free-flowing, poetic-like, and nuanced Aramaic, this word might mean hundreds of legitimate things to the speaker and each person hearing those words. Exactly how it was meant to mean may not at all be like how we have been interpreting things to be for hundreds and hundreds of years. We have traditionally based our understanding of the New Testament on the Latin Vulgate, which is itself a rendition only of the earliest Greek Gospels which tried to put Jesus' free-flowing Aramaic teachings into lock-clad Greek and then into Latin.

There is a new version of the New Testament, titled the *New* New Testament, in which the Scribe who wrote it all down tells the rest of us that Jesus and the original authors gave him these words in vision. Think what you may about that, if you read it, you will be impressed.

Most readers think "What do I care rather it is real or it is crazy; it really *moves* me to be a much better person."

In this *New* New Testament, Jesus emphasizes that he doesn't care very much what we believe if we only love each other as he loves us and as God (his and our "Dad") loves him and loves us.

Religion/spirituality was not meant to be an adhesion to a series of doctrines where you would be punished if you stepped outside of their beliefs or social boundaries (sin!). Religion was supposed to be a philosophy of life that led toward becoming more God-like. It's fluid, changing, and adapting to the individual at different times and places. It honors the fact that we are here on this planet to make mistakes.

Much of this follow-on from Dr. Newton's work is my own, but it coincides with and compliments that of Dr. Newton. I can find hardly any relevance between the Medieval perspective and Dr. Newton's work. Dr. Newton did not question, "What is a soul?" Rather, he asked, "Where is the soul ("that which is 'us' when the body is gone") going? What is it doing here that helps that projected journey?"

For Dr. Newton's subjects, no matter how often a person may have made a less-than-best decision and created for themselves and/or for others a difficult time here on earth (i.e., "hell on wheels"), those former decisions and acts no longer count as negative (indeed, even as "sin"). That is the case the moment that person, at his next time confronting that same type of decision, arrives at the inclination to do something different than before (because those past decisions had not brought happiness but a sense of emptiness and pain) and then decides to do something he had felt as a tug from his soul to act kindly or lovingly. That is how this plane is supposed to work!

How can there be any such thing as "sin" if sin is defined as walking away from God? Our PURPOSE in coming here is to confront CHALLENGES (otherwise known as "things that need to be made better" or "problems"). That is why we are born over and over again to be confronted with problems because problems are the way we grow fastest. We choose to grow as fast as possible.

So, to come into earth with our perfect (but not completely formed) soul into a body subject to dog-eat-dog, DNA, and survival of the fittest means that we are going to be tempted – and fail – by doing what our animal body wants. We will find that those wants are not satisfying, and eventually we will decide to try our divine side's tug to be kind and loving. When we do, BINGO! We find something *THAT WORKS*. We discover *that* pleases us because *that is who we truly are*. When that happens, all those temptations to which we succumbed to are revealed to be *blessings*, because they seared onto our experiences and memories the permeating understanding of another aspect of our divine origin. We are NOT punished for that which we came here for.

More than a third of all Americans have believed in reincarnation for more than forty years. It is no longer just an "eastern" belief.

In fact, a great many of the early Church Fathers believed in reincarnation, but it was drummed out of Christianity when Augustine, enormously influential in the Fourth Century, disfavored it. When early Christians fled their homes during the Roman invasion of Jerusalem in the mid-first century, many went to upper Egypt. Centuries later, many secret manuscripts were found in 1945, the Dead Sea Scrolls. These writings affirmed the existence of the doctrine of reincarnation taught among the early Christians and Jews.

It is said in Christianity today that at the Second Council of Constantinople in 553 A.D., the idea of reincarnation was rejected. It was not. Although reincarnation was not rejected outright, those early Church Fathers who were accused of teaching the idea of reincarnation (a significant number, including Justin Martyr [AD 100-165], St. Clement of Alexandria [AD 150-220], and Origen [AD 185-254]) had their works banned. Before that, the concept of reincarnation had been hotly debated. To this day, there is no Christian prohibition to a belief in reincarnation.

Moreover, how does one reconcile various passages in the Gospels about reincarnation?

First, they asked Jesus, "Who sinned, this man or his parents, that he should be born blind?" How could he have sinned before he was born blind if there was no reincarnation?

Secondly, Jesus asked, "Who do they say I am?" Some said John the Baptist and some said Elijah. "Come again." What's this? Sounds like reincarnation to me.

Thirdly, Jesus said a man cannot enter heaven unless he be "born again."

The previously mentioned *New* New Testament (subtitled BEYOND MORTAL) is much more explicit and much more often in its testimony supporting reincarnation.

People can wiggle their way through contorted explanations of the references in both versions of the New Testament, but a belief in reincarnation is the most direct conclusion. It was perhaps not mentioned directly because it may have been assumed. Nobody mentions going to the bathroom in the New Testament either; it too was assumed as understood.

"Soul" is just a specific name created for a specific meaning, and it basically reflects who we are in expressing ourselves through our minds, our emotions, and our wills. I prefer "life force," because it is draped less with references to concepts of old that we now know to be false because each word in "life" and "force" has meaning on its own and brings that meaning compounded to Life Force. It's a force reaching from beyond ourselves and giving us unique characteristics which enable us to seek to be like this Loving Consciousness that we know to be Ultimate Perfection.

No soul ever has a life apart from God ("All-Loving Awareness" or "Loving Consciousness") because God is the constant source of *all* life. Anything separate from God is either a competitor god – little or big (Like how can there be multiple "gods?" ... who created them?) –

or evaporates at the moment of "separation." That is why if everything exists WITHIN God and is an Individuated Manifestation of God, then every soul is perfect ... just not yet fully developed.

I can look into a mirror and not doubt that there is a "me" inside that body. That "me" is at the core of my human body/spirit. This may not be explicit in the findings of Dr. Newton, but it coincides completely with his findings.

No Such Thing as Death

When a soul again returns to a pure energy state in the spirit world, it no longer feels hate, anger, envy, jealousy, and similar emotions. It has come to earth to experience these sorts of emotions and learn from them. But after departing from Earth, do souls feel any sadness for what they have left behind? Certainly, souls carry nostalgia for the good times in all their past physical lives. This is tempered by a state of blissful omniscience and such a heightened sense of well-being that souls feel more alive than when they were on earth.

There are two types of negative emotions that Dr. Newton has noted within souls, both of which involve a form of sadness. One of them is karmic guilt for making very poor choices, especially when others were hurt by these actions. The other form is *not* melancholy, dejection, or mournful unhappiness in the way life has gone on without them since their departure. Rather, sadness in souls comes from a longing to reunite with the Source of their existence. All souls, regardless of their level of development, have this longing to seek perfection for the same reason. *The motivating factor for those souls who come to earth is growth.* It is a soul's destiny to search for truth in their experiences to gain wisdom.

From now on, on the other side and because of the nature of soul duality, they are quite capable of carrying on multiple tasks at one time.

Death is like waking up after a long sleep where you had just a muddled awareness. Death only exchanges one reality for another, in fact a more aware, more sensitive, more joyful one in the long continuum of existence.

Souls often leave their physical bodies seconds before a violent death.

When we die, we enter into a sort of tunnel, which is beautiful, full of caring and power.

Let's stop for just a second and clear something up to get rid of a misconception. This "other side," heretofore referred to as "heaven," is not a place where disincarnate bodies sing hymns of worship to God all day and night to worship "his" majesty. That sounds incredibly boring. Rather, according to Dr. Newton's reports from thousands of witnesses, it is a place of unmitigated joy, community, intimate relationships, happiness, friendship, "love," and humor. There is absolutely no discord there. Given our choice, we would never leave if we didn't want to accelerate our appreciation of who we are and what we have. To do that, we choose to come here from "time to time" (there is no "time" on the other side).

Dr. Newton states that he is not at all attracted to the rigid stair-stop quality of exactly seven planes of existence, from low to high, which come from Eastern spiritual philosophy. This is because none of his thousands of clients ever saw any evidence of these planes. That is a human failing to label concepts as a means of codification. These states are necessarily inhibitors. Subjects in a higher state of consciousness indicate that upon death, we go directly from one astral plane around the earth to the gateway into the spirit world. It does not matter if the subject is a young soul or a highly advanced older soul. Right after death, they all pass through a dense atmosphere of light around the astral plane of Earth. This light has patches of darkish gray but no impenetrable black zones. Many describe the tunnel effect. All souls from earth then quickly move into the bright light of the spirit world. This is a single ethereal space without zones or barriers around it.

People in hypnosis report that within the astral plane surrounding Earth, alternate or coexistent realities are part of our physical world. Apparently, within these realities, non-material beings can be seen by some people in our physical reality. Multitudes of interdimensional spheres are used by souls for training and recreation from the spirit world. All spatial zones have vibrational properties that allow for soul passage only when their energy waves are attuned to the proper frequency. If what people tell him has validity, etheric beings would be capable of existing in different realities within the same astral plane surrounding Earth – indeed on Earth itself.

One such client was an old soul who, while in a deep trance, told him that fairy folks were here long before the rise of our civilizations and have never left. Most of us do not see them today, as in ancient times, because they are so old their density has become very light while our earth bodies still have heavy energy. She said that while a rock has a 1-D (density), a tree would be a 2-D and our bodies are at the 3-D level. Thus, the beings of nature would be invisible with transparency registering between 4-D and 6-D. If we could look at the Earth with X-ray vision, it might resemble a series of overlaid, clear plastic topographical sheets. These vibrational energy layers vary in density and denote alternate realities. Certain gifted people might be able to see within these layers, but most of us are unable to do so.

Much of our folklore comes from the memories that souls have of their experiences in other physical and mental worlds. What they have to say about these experiences while under hypnosis conforms in some respects to the myths and legends of Earth.

At the moment of our death, our soul rises out of its host body. If the soul is older and has experience from many former lives, it knows immediately it has been set free and is going home. These advanced souls need no one to greet them. However, most souls Dr. Newton works with are met by guides just outside Earth's astral plane. A young soul, or a child who has died, may be a little disoriented until someone comes closer to ground level for them. There are souls, however, who choose to remain at the scene of their death for a while. But most wish to leave at once.

As they move further away from Earth, souls would experience an increasingly brilliant light around them. Some will briefly see a grayish darkness and pass through what they sense is a tunnel or portal. The differences between these two phenomena depend upon the exit speed of the soul, which in turn relates to their experience. The pulling sensation from our guides (more on "guides" later) may be gentle or forceful depending upon the soul's maturity and capacity for rapid change. In the early stages of their exit, all souls encounter a "wispy cloudiness" around them that soon becomes clear, enabling them to look off into a vast distance. This is the moment when the average soul sees a ghostly form of energy coming toward them. This figure may be a loving soulmate or two. But more often than not, it is his or her guide. In circumstances where we are met by a spouse or friend who has passed on before us, our guide is also close by. As such, they can take over the transition process. In all his years of research, Dr. Newton never had a single subject who was met by a major religious figure such as Jesus, Buddha, or Mohammad.

When we cross over and are met by our guides, Dr. Newton found that the techniques these guides use fall into two categories:

Envelopment: Returning souls are completely cloaked by a large circular mass of their guide's powerful energy. As the soul and guide come together, the soul feels as though they both are encased in a bubble. This is the more common method which subjects describe as pure ecstasy.

The Focus Effect: This alternate procedure of initial contact is administered a little differently. As the guide approaches, energy is applied to certain points at the edges of the soul's etheric body (the etheric body is the thought form that sets the soul in the earthly physical body) from any direction of the guide's choosing. We might be taken by the hand or held by the tops of our shoulders from a side position. Healing begins from a specific point of the etheric body in the form of a brushing caress followed by deep penetration.

The etheric or soul body is, in more detailed description, an outline of our old physical body which souls take into the spirit world. Essentially, it is an imprint of a human form we have not shed yet like the skin of a reptile. This is not a permanent condition, although we might naturally create it later as a colorful, luminescent shape of energy.

By the time souls become reoriented again to the place they call home, their earthliness has now changed. They are no longer quite human in the way we think of a human being with a particular emotional, temperamental, and physical makeup. For instance, they don't grieve about their recent physical death in the way their loved ones will.

Right after death, souls suddenly feel different because they are no longer encumbered by a temporary host body with a brain and central nervous system. Some do take longer to adjust than others.

When souls arrive at the gateway to the spirit world with energy that is in a deteriorated state, some of our guides engage in emergency healing. This is both a physical and mental healing exercise that takes place before the soul moves any further into the spirit world.

As we move away from the tunnel, we encounter layers of stratified light with echoes of vibrational music (the "energy of the universe").

Guides and important people in our lives are always available to greet us. Exactly the right people greet us at just the right moment, but not all people who greet us in our immediate past life will be in our cluster.

Then, the soul rides a beam of light which pulls it to a **place of healing**, and then the soul goes in resonance. In this place of healing, souls are examined by their guides. This is a vessel of healing, of pure (what seems like) liquid energy. **We are bathed in a shower of directed energy.**

Immediately after that shower, souls have a **rehabilitation stage** (especially with younger souls) which involves a substantial counseling session with one's guide. Past life is debriefed, emotions are released, and readjustment is made to the spirit life.

(There is no punishment for suicide. You will just have wasted a lot of time and will have to go back and start that part over again. Suicides go back to the spirit world dejected. However, if a suicide checks out because of chronic physical pain or almost total incapacity, everyone has a more accepting view of this.)

Orientation periods with our guides, which take place before joining our cluster group, vary between souls and between different lives from the same soul. This is a quiet time for counseling, with the opportunity to vent any frustrations we have about the life that just ended. Orientation is intended to be an initial debriefing session with gentle probing by perceptive, caring teacher guides.

Staying in Contact with the Deceased

When a person dies, they will stay around until they can give comfort to those they love. Sometimes, they penetrate their loved one's mind for days until they can break through and leave a measure of comfort.

The best thing those grieving the loss of a loved one can do is to take a piece of jewelry or clothing that belonged to the departed to a mutually familiar place. One would then hold it while quietly opening your mind and blanking out all irrelevant thoughts.

One of the ways the newly-departed soul uses to reach people who love them is through the dream state. The grief that has overwhelmed them is temporarily pushed out of a frontal position in their thoughts when they are asleep. Unfortunately, the person who is grieving will all too often wake up from a dream that could have contained a message and instead allow it to slip away from memory without writing anything down.

Disincarnate spirits are very selective in their use of our dream sequences. Most dreams are not profound. Mythic memories contain other information about the lives we led as intelligent flying or water creatures on other planets. Some of our greatest revelations come from the episodic dreams of events, places, and behavior patterns emanating from experiences before we acquired our present body.

Some recently discarnate souls will latch on to a dream of a loved one, waiting for just the right one to come along to make it a vivid dream that becomes a great influence. The dream can move from an unconscious to a conscious reality in the dreamer's mind. Other dream influencers can create and fully implant a wholly new dream in the dreamer's mind.

When souls have difficulty reaching the mind of a troubled adult, they might resort to using children as conduits for their messages. Children are more receptive to spirits because they have not been conditioned to doubt or resist the supernatural. Frequently, the young person chosen as a conduit is a family member of the departed.

Souls don't give up easily on us. Another way spirits touch people is through environmental settings associated with their memory.

The person on earth has to listen very closely to hear their departed loved one. There is the need to be alone and very still, to allow the mind to go free from the body.

Departing spouses only want their surviving mates to be happy and loved. People who have had long, happy first marriages and then lose a spouse make excellent candidates for a successful second marriage. This is a tribute to the first relationship. Having other relationships does not lessen nor dishonor our first love. It only validates that love, providing a state of healthy acceptance reached in between.

Settling In, on the Other Side

Before we go on, one caution. *Worldly intelligence does not equate to soul development.* You simply cannot tell by observing a very smart person whether he or she is an advanced soul or not. Intelligence is a brain function. On the other side, we will know everything we want to know, and we will appear as positively brilliant – were we just on earth.

When souls join their bodies on earth, they only bring a partial amount of their total energy. They may bring 50% of their energy with them, which means that 50% remains behind. Sometimes they may only bring as little as 25% or 30% and that proves inadequate to the challenges on earth. Sometimes they bring up to 75% of 80% and it overblows their mortal capacities. No matter the amount of energy brought to earth, a certain percentage remains behind. When a person dies on earth, those energies must be reunited as part of the reassociation process.

Unless there are complications from a past life, most souls reacquire the balance of their energy at one of the three primary spiritual stations: near the **gateway**, **during orientation**, or after returning to their **soul group**. The advanced souls usually disembark only at the final stop on their journey home.

Receiving our energy at the gateway is not really a common occurrence. This is probably due to the initiation of recovery by a shower of healing near the gate.

The usual way most souls reunite with the balance of their energy is after returning to a cluster group. A subject put it this way, "It is smoother for me to reunite with myself after I arrive at home base with my friends. Here the infusion of my rested energy can be assimilated at my own pace. When I am ready, I go get it myself."

One subject said: "Sometimes I like to wait until after my council meeting because I don't want the fresh energy to dilute the memories and feelings I had in the life just lived. If I did infuse myself (by taking in reserve energy), that former life would be less real to me. I want my thought to be centered on answering questions about my work in that body with a clear, lucid memory of each event. I want to retain every emotional feeling I had of these events as they occurred so I can better describe why I took certain actions. My friends don't like to do this, but I can always recharge and rest later."

A cluster group to which we belong has 3 to 25 souls, with an average size of about 15. There is a oneness there and you feel that you are joyfully *home*. There is no suspicion. Instead, there is complete openness and acceptance. We are overjoyed to be back with our friends. You don't choose to know intimately about people in other clusters, because you are so involved with your own. You are especially careful about infringing upon other souls in other clusters because you respect the work they do, as they do you.

Homecoming is a joyous interlude, especially following a physical life where there might not have been much karmic contact with our intimate soulmates. Most of Dr. Newton's subjects tell him they are welcomed back with hugs, laughter, and much humor, which he finds to be the hallmark of a life in the spirit world. The really effusive groups who have planned elaborate celebrations for the returning soul may also suspend all their other activities.

Homecoming can take place in two types of settings A few souls might briefly meet a returning soul at the gateway and then leave in favor of a guide who takes them through some preliminary orientation. More commonly, the welcoming committee waits until the soul returns to their spirit group. This group may be isolated in a classroom, gathered around the steps of a temple, sat in a garden, or the returning soul could encounter many groups in a study hall atmosphere. Souls who pass by other clusters on the way to their own berth often remark that other souls with whom they have been associated in past lives will look up and acknowledge their return with a smile or wave.

In the spirit world, educational placement depends on the level of soul development. Simply because a soul has been incarnating on earth since the Stone Age is no guarantee of high attainment. Dr. Newton often remarked about a client who took 4,000 years of past lives finally to conquer jealousy.

Generally, the composition of a group of souls is made up of beings at about the same level of advancement, although they have their individual strengths and shortcomings. These attributes give the group balance. Souls assist one another with the cognitive aspects of absorbing information from life experiences as well as reviewing the way they handled the feelings and emotions of their host bodies directly related to those experiences. Every aspect of a life is dissected, even to the extent of reverse role-playing in the group, to bring greater awareness.

Cluster groups may want to connect with each other. Often this activity involves older souls who have made many friends from other groups with whom they have been associated over hundreds of past lives.

What Is Your Cluster and What Do You Do There?

A cluster is like a spiritual school, but it's one that is extremely pleasant and looked forward to. To start, when you get to your cluster, you go to the Council of Masters for an examination of your past life. These are not prosecutorial, but they are direct. They are kind and they help us evaluate what we could have done better. A couple of them are more involved with me than the others. My guide is always with me to help when I feel I get left behind in the conversation. The people in each cluster have a familiarity with us like a family does, but they're much more intimate. We are united with this cluster group for all eternity. We come back to earth together in different roles – usually in the form of brothers, sisters, friends, close relatives ... and not-so-often parents. In our clusters, we study spiritual books, which are living pictures usually of our past lives and alternatives. Souls in a cluster help each other to study these books and gain insights. We study together. We can also go and help others in other clusters. After we adapt once again to our cluster, we then like to go out to recreational areas with others.

Secondary groups (1,000 or more) form the next and final level of acquaintance ... much less familiar than in our own cluster.

Leisure Activities and Physical Love in the Spirit World

Life between lives is hardly all work and no play. Hundreds of subjects talk about what they do after their training.

The poignancy of tasting food and drink, touching human bodies, experiencing the senses of walking the deserts, climbing mountains, and swimming in the seas of Earth all remain with the soul. An eternal mind can reminisce about the motor movements and sensory pleasures of a human vessel and all the feelings it generated. Naturally, souls would want to maintain these planetary memories by re-creating their former bodies in the spirit world.

The desire for time alone in the spirit world comes from an intense need to dwell within the sacred confines of pure thought to try and touch the Source from which they sprang. Some souls come to Earth as invisible beings between lives so they can re-experience former physical environments. The only problem with this is that they must return to chronological time, which means these souls are caught up with change since they were last here. Some won't come back for this reason – things change, and they prefer their memories. Those who return just bring enough energy – often about 5% – to be enjoying themselves without being seen.

People are often curious if souls can have intimate physical relations with their re-created bodies. If good sex originates in the mind, then the pure soul has all the benefits without the physical inhibitors. No self-pretense is possible in the spirit world. There is a loss of tactile sensation by not being within a dense physical body that has a nervous system. At any rate in the spiritual recreation of a human body, the lack of full sensory sensation is more than made up for by the erotic power of two minds that are completely joined.

Love is a desire for full unification with the object of that love. Spirits have the capability between lives to express love even more intimately than on Earth. Even so, some souls are still motivated by establishing the scenes of former lives where their love blossomed. A major incentive for many souls to reincarnate is the pleasures of physical expression in the biological form.

During their long apprenticeship of training, souls can study and practice many arts. They can enter a space of soul transformation. The young souls are introduced to certain arts here that might interest them while the older souls can hone their existing skills further.

The **Space of Transformation** is not limited to, but mainly is, permitting souls to get inside the energy of animals. Here, the soul can become any animate or inanimate object familiar to them. To capture the essence of all living and even nonliving things on Earth, souls can meld with multiple substances. This would include fire, gas, and liquids. They may also become totally amorphous to meld with a feeling or emotion and become one with that state.

The Space of Transformation is often used for recreation for average or new souls. But all these activities have the potential to go far beyond recreation for most souls.

One subject stated, "I learn to manipulate my energy rather than absorb pain. The energy belt of compassion is like a liquid pool where I can swim and become part of the emotion in an experience which is so subjective I cannot describe it to you. It assists me in working on calmness within a sea of adversity. It is wondrous ... it is ... alive."

Dr. Newton states, "Whether these psychic pools of concentrated energy, which appear to transform souls for a time, are real or simulated from my frame of reference is moot. This is because while my clients see the spirit world as ultimate reality, they call this space one of altered reality. There is one constant criterion that helps me differentiate these concepts in my mind. Working models of reality which are temporary and will eventually die are illusory. The eternal world of the soul that analyzes and evaluates this process appears to my subjects as a permanent state of consciousness. The Space of Transformation is a creation for spiritual development."

Souls in heaven also enjoy **Dancing**, **Music**, and **Games**. Many also enjoy **acrobatics**, which are different than human acrobatics. "We retain our oval, or elongated shapes of pure energy. We set up an energy field resembling a kind of trampoline to be used for tumbling in relays. It includes a dance form which is too hard to describe, but it's all done with a great deal of laughter and fun. This movement during recreation draws us closer together." These activities may be combined with comedy skits. Souls who engage in these forms of entertainment love to poke fun at each other.

Other recreational activities, such as **Art** and **Composition**, are pursued quietly and individually. The practice of **Music** and **Sculpture** may also be pursued alone or collectively. Sculpting energy to design structural objects and the creation of small life forms is not really considered recreational. They represent an integral part of task-oriented classroom instruction, although these activities can be overlapped with leisure time.

Music, meanwhile, is in a special category on its own with almost universal soul appeal. Unlike on Earth, where so many of us are unable to learn to play a musical instrument or sing, souls seem to be able to engage in these activities effortlessly. Melodic sounds are often heard throughout the spirit world by Dr. Newton's subjects in spaces that are not recreational. Within the context of R&R, music is enjoyed by souls directly or interwoven into subtle frameworks for drama, dancing, and even games.

More than any other medium, music uplifts the soul with ranges of notes far beyond what we know on Earth. There seems to be no limit to the sounds used in the creation of music in the spirit world. People in deep hypnosis explain that musical thought is the language of the soul. The composition and transmission of harmonic resonance appears to relate to the formation and presentation of spiritual language. Far beyond musical communication, spiritual harmonics are the building blocks of energy creation and soul unification.

When spirits apply themselves to instruments and voice sounds, it's wonderful. It's not stray notes. The harmonic meshing of musical energy reverberates throughout the spirit world with indescribable sounds. There, you have so much talent because every soul has the capability for the perfection of musical sound. There is high motivation to do so. Souls love this form of recreation, especially if they wanted to sing on Earth back then but instead sounded like frogs.

Music is so important in the spirit world because it takes souls to new mental levels by moving their energy and communicating in unison with large numbers of other souls.

Moreover, there are **Spiritual Games** that are not played with the objective that somebody wins while others lose. Games are vigorous and carefree at the same time. Guides encourage game participation as a means of practicing energy movement, dexterity, and group thought transmission. On the other hand, there are subjects whose groups do not participate in games in the spirit world. Their separateness is always respected. This is especially true with the more advanced souls who are so engaged in other forms of energy training that playing games would be a detraction. Souls do not seem to play golf, because it is too self-centered. It's the case with tennis as well for the same reason.

Council of Elders

After the initial orientation, the guide prepares you for a session (not a trial or a courtroom) with three to seven Council of Masters (Elders) who analyze your past life, primarily based upon *intent* rather than *actions*. A step or two above our guides, these ascended masters are the most advanced identifiable entities Dr. Newton's still-incarnating clients see in the spirit world. Human subjects give them different human names such as the Old Ones, the Sacred Masters, the Venerables, and pragmatic titles like the Examiners or the Committee. The two most common names are Council and Elders.

Even senior guides are thought to be a couple of steps below the development level of the omnipotent beings who make up the council. Similar to the Old Ones, they have more specific responsibilities toward the life evaluation of souls. They do not extend "familiarity" to those souls they attend. All souls see their Council of Elders as godly. The Elders are bathed in a bright light, and the whole setting has an aura of divinity. They validate the souls' feelings about the source of creation.

Souls appear before their council right after finishing an incarnation, and many report that they will visit them a second time just before rebirth.

Rather than stages of punishment, we go through stages of self-enlightenment. Yet, large segments of human society are unable to shake off the nagging feeling, built over thousands of years of cultural conditioning, that judgment and punishment must exist in some form in the afterlife as it does on Earth.

There will be those who feel accountability towards a Council of Elders may not be all that comfortable. The Epicureans of this world – those devoted solely to uninhibited pleasure in life while paying little attention to the plight of others – might also be unhappy with the truth of life in the spirit world. The same can be said for the Iconoclasts, who are opposed to authority of any kind, moral or otherwise.

The spirit world is a place of order, and the Council of Elders exemplifies justice. They are not the ultimate source of divine authority, but they appear to represent the last station of beings responsible for souls still incarnating on Earth. These wise beings have great compassion for human weakness, and they demonstrate infinite patience with our faults. We will be given many second chances in our future lives. They won't be lives of easy karmic choices. Otherwise, we would learn nothing by coming to Earth.

The descriptions of the form and procedure of council meetings are very consistent among all hypnosis subjects. A great majority of subjects visualize a dome design for the chamber of the Council of Elders. They see the chamber structure as a manifestation of a holy place on Earth. The guide stands behind the subject to his left. This is because the left side of the brain is weaker than the right side, and the first council meeting seems to be only hours after death. The soul is still feeling the effects of his human body, with the guide serving to help thoughts from falling out the left side. During these hearings, council members might communicate with each other in a rapid pitch of high and low vibrations. The average soul misses most of this sort of intercommunication between elders.

The object of the council meetings is not to demean the souls who come before them or to punish them for their shortcomings. The purpose of the Elders is to question the soul to help them achieve their goals in the next lifetime. Every soul has an awareness of the inquiry format for their life review, although they likewise know that no two council visits will be the same. At meetings for the younger souls, Dr. Newton noticed both guides and council members were especially indulgent and solicitous. Directed questioning by these spiritual masters toward the subjects is both firm and benevolent.

What souls feel for their council is reverence. Souls themselves are their own severest critics. Evaluations by our soul group companions are far more acerbic than any council Elder, although our peers do lace their criticism with humor. The Elders have a way of making the souls who come before them feel welcome almost at once. One of the most obvious differences between a courtroom on Earth and a spiritual gathering of grandmasters is the fact that everyone in the chamber is telepathic. Thus, all in attendance know the whole truth about every aspect of our conduct and the choices we made in the past life. Deception is impossible.

Regardless of the number of times we continue to make the same mistakes, our council has enormous patience with us. However, we have much less patience with ourselves.

The council is looking to see if the inner immortal character of our soul maintained its integrity in terms of values, ideals, and actions during incarnation. They want to know if we were submerged by our host body, or did we shine through? *The council is not so concerned about how many times we fall down in our progress through life. They are concerned about whether we have the courage to pick ourselves up and finish strong.*

Most advanced subjects, along with large numbers of intermediate souls, see their councils as androgynous. Younger souls see more men, and this is probably cultural. Spirit guides, on the other hand, are represented equally as male and female between clients.

The typical soul sees between three to seven members on their council, while an advanced soul might have anywhere from seven to 12 Elders. More members are present for older souls because the more experience we have, the more specialized help we can use. That which you gain from each difficult life is what you gain for all eternity. The vast majority of souls do not feel close to the Elders on their councils. They have reverence and veneration for them, but they do not have the deep affection they display toward their spiritual guides.

What souls hear in their minds is "We are not here to judge you, punish you, or to override your thoughts. We want you to look at yourself through our eyes, if you can. That means to forgive yourself.

This is the most challenging aspect of your time with us, because it is our desire that you accept yourself for who you are with the same unconditional love we have for you. We are here to support your work on Earth." There are no simple acts to the council. As we move through life, there are many gestures between uplifting people. They may be so momentary that we are not conscious of them at the time. In the spirit world, nothing is insignificant. No act goes unrecorded.

The Presence

The source of the origin of souls is all about them in the spirit world. The more advanced explain that all souls will eventually coalesce back into conjunction with the source of purple light. However, there is a place in the spirit world where a being which is superior to the Elders is evident to the still-incarnating souls, and that place is at council meetings. During the time the soul is meeting with the Council of Elders, there is the overwhelming feeling of an even higher force which is simply called "the Presence." Many subjects state, "This is as close to God as we get." More advanced souls don't think the Presence is actually God. To them, it is a deified entity or entities with capabilities immensely superior to those on the council. Everyone agrees that the Presence is there to assist the work of the council:

> ◈ "When I am in the council chamber the Presence oversees the Elders with its pulsating violet light. Sometimes it turns to a bright silver to calm and purify my mind."

> ◈ "The Presence is above and in back of the council. Only with difficulty can I look up at this power. I feel its sanctity so strongly that I don't think I should try to look at it directly during the council meeting. If I did, I could not stay focused on the Elders."

◈ "The council seems to acknowledge the Presence without being too deferential to it in such a way as to slow down the proceedings. I think it intended that my council and I pay attention to each other. Still, I have the impression that the magnitude of all this combined intelligent energy is designed just for me at the moment my guide, the elders, and the Presence are keepers of the wisdom behind my experiences."

◈ "The Presence represents a purity of energy which assists the council on my behalf. I believe that the council needs the help of the Presence because it has been so long since they themselves incarnated in biological form. The pure wisdom of this energy allows both the council and myself to see more clearly where we all should be going."

◈ "The brilliance and drawing power of the Presence is a calling... an eagerness... directed at everyone in the chamber for all of us to join it someday. It is like a parent waiting for us to grow up and unite with it in adult understanding."

If one were a member of the council, the next place they could look forward to going is to the place of Oneness, the many who are One ... the creation center where the creators of new souls shape light energy for certain functions. This is where they help the young ones grow to find their unique identity. This Oneness is divineness but is probably not the ultimate deity of all universes and all dimensions connecting these universes. This may be the same force of which the Presence is a part. It's massive but soft, powerful yet gentle. There is a breath, a whisper of sound so pure. This sound creates all, including light and energy. According to a subject, "I feel the sound holds this structure ... and ... makes it move ... shifting and undulating ... creating everything.

It is a reverberating deep bell ... then a high-pitched pure humming ... like an echo of ... a mother, full of love, singing to her child."

The Council of Elders exists within a reality of deeper meaning beyond the conception of souls still coming to Earth. To many, the Presence seems not to be a "who" but "that which is." For others, the Presence is an entity that functions as an equalizer, harmonizing the greater awareness of Elders with the lesser awareness of the souls who come before them. This effect causes the council chamber to breathe with synchronized energy.

One Level V (see the "levels" of spiritual attainment a few chapters below) who had sat on a council said, "It was like being inside the soul in front of you. What you feel is much more than empathy toward someone who has just come back from a life. You are really in their shoes. The Presence gives you the power to feel everything the soul feels at the moment. This prism of light from the Presence touches every council member in this way."

Within the texture of any soul evaluation by one's council, there runs the thread of divine forgiveness. The Elders provide a forum of both inquiry and compassion. They display their desire to bolster the confidence of the soul for their future endeavors. One soul said, "When I leave them, I feel they have absorbed all my self-doubt and cleansed me."

Journey Onward

After our individual meeting with the Council of Elders, we then leave the place of orientation and **join an enormous number of souls into a kind of receiving station** (like mass transit). We will be going to a more unified celestial field. Souls are excited and dazzled by this spirit world opening up to them. The most outstanding characteristic of the spirit world is a continuous feeling of a powerful mental force directing everything in uncanny harmony. People say this is a place of pure thought.

It is at this point that **souls begin to anticipate meeting others** who wait for them. They have met a few souls as they came in at first, but none of them are those whom they want to see. They only have to think of the person to have that person appear in their soul-mind telepathically. Those souls who are actively incarnate in two or more bodies are rarely there to greet you. Sometimes, this disappoints you. But when you figure out why, you are fine with that reality.

There is a non-visual affinity, and everyone can see and understand this communication. For those who want a private conversation, they must be present to each other. They must embrace in a joining spirit to communicate privately.

Souls then go from this receiving station into **what seems like a giant river with a multitude of souls flowing and being pulled in a unified direction**. Gradually, we are then pulled into smaller tributaries, and we slow down. When we get there, we can drift. There are thousands upon thousands of groupings, and souls get pulled to the cluster of their friends.

Regardless of the specific energy treatment received by the soul at the gateway to the spirit world, most if not all returning souls will continue to some sort of healing station before finally joining their groups. All but the most advanced souls crossing back into the spirit world are met by benevolent spirits who make contact with their positive energy and escort needy souls to quiet recovery areas. It is only the more highly developed souls, with energy patterns that are still strong after their incarnations, who return directly to their regular activities. The more advanced souls appear to get over hardship more quickly than others after a life.

Most recovery areas for the returning soul involve some kind of orientation back to the spirit world. It may be intense or moderate in scope depending upon the condition of the soul. This usually includes a preliminary debriefing of the life just completed. Much more in-depth counseling will take place later with guides in group conferences and with our Council of Elders. The surroundings of recovery areas are identifiable earthly settings created out of our memories and what spiritual guides feel will promote healing. Orientation environments are not the same after each of our lives.

Chapter 5
The Growth Process of Souls

The Birth of Souls

(Note: We are humans trying to express the creation of souls in the spirit world, and so we use earthly terms which will not seem real to the true conditions of the spirit world ... but ... human words are all we have!)

From a subject: "My soul was created out of a great irregular cloudy mass. I was expelled as a time particle of energy from this intense white light. The pulsations send out hailstorms of soul matter. Some fall back and are reabsorbed but I continued outward and was being carried along in a stream with others like me. The next thing I knew, I was in a bright enclosed area with very loving beings taking care of me.

"I remember being in a nursery of some sort where we were like unhatched eggs in a beehive. When I acquired more awareness, I learned I was in the nursery world of Uras. I don't know how I got there. I was like an egg in embryonic fluid waiting to be fertilized, and I sensed there were many other cells of young lights who were coming awake with me. There was a group of mothers, beautiful and loving, who ... pierced our membrane sacs and opened us. There were swirling currents of intense, nurturing lights around us and I could hear music. My awareness began with curiosity. Soon, I was taken from Uras and joined other children in a different setting."

And from another subject, an advanced soul, who was a "mother" taking care of new souls: "We help the new ones emerge. We facilitate early maturation ... by being warm, gentle, and caring. We welcome them. [The surroundings are ...] gas-like ... a honeycomb of cells with swirling currents of energy above. There is intense light. [There is a beehive-like structure,] although the nursery itself is a vast emporium without seeming to be limited by outside dimensions. The new souls have their own incubator cells where they stay until their growth is sufficient to be moved away from the emporium. [An Incubator Mother first sees the new souls when] ... we are in the delivery suite, which is a part of the nursery at one end of the emporium. Then, newly arrived ones are conveyed as small masses of white energy encased in a gold sac. They move slowly in a majestic, orchestrated line of progression toward us ... At our end of the emporium under an archway the entire wall is filled with a molten mass of high-intensity energy and ... vitality. It feels as if it's energized by an amazing love force rather than a discernible heat source. The mass pulsates and undulates in a beautiful flowing motion. Its color is like that on the inside of your eyelids if you were to look through closed eyes at the sun on a bring day.

"From the mass a swelling begins, never exactly from the same site twice. The swelling increases and pushes outward, becoming a formless bulge. The separation is a wondrous moment. A new soul is born. It's totally alive with an energy and distinctness of its own."

Another one of Dr. Newton's Level V subjects states, "I see an egg-shaped mass with energy flowing out and back in. When it expands, new soul energy fragments are spawned. When the bulge contracts, I think it pulls back those souls which were not successfully spawned. For some reason, these fragments could not make it on to the next step of individuality."

The responsibilities of an Incubator Mother are to hover around the hatchlings to towel-dry them after opening their golden sacs (a form of hugging new white energy). Their progression is slow because this allows the Incubator Mothers to embrace their tiny energy in a timeless, exquisite fashion. One Mother said "Through us – not from us – comes a life force of all-knowing love and knowledge. What we pass on with our vibrations during the drying of new energy is ... the essence of a beginning, a hopefulness of future accomplishment. The mothers call it ... 'the love hug.' This involves instilling thoughts of what they are and what they can become. When we enfold a new soul in a love hug, it infuses this being with our understanding and compassion."

The new soul has an individual character upon arrival, although the new souls do not yet know who they are. The Incubator Mothers bring nurturing. They are announcing to the hatchling that it is time to begin. By sparking its energy, they bring to the soul an awareness of its existence. This is the time of the awakening.

"Each soul is unique in its totality of characteristics created by a perfection that I cannot begin to describe. What I can tell you is that no two souls are alike – none ever! ... I have the sense that there is a powerful Presence on the other side of the archway who is managing things. If there is a key to the energy patterns, we do not need to know of this."

Dr. Newton asked a particular Incubator Mother if she worked only with souls coming to Earth. "Yes, but they could go to all kinds of places. Only a fraction come to Earth. There are many physical worlds similar to Earth. We call them pleasure worlds and suffering worlds. I know that souls who come to worlds such as Earth need to be strong and resilient because of the pain they have to endure along with the joy ... Perfection is there ... with the newly created. Maturity begins by the shattering of innocence with new soul, not because they are originally flawed. Overcoming obstacles makes them stronger, but the acquired imperfections will never be totally erased until all souls are joined together – when incarnation ends. ***Incarnations will end on Earth when all races, nationalities unite as one.***"

The universe we live in may die before souls are finished. It doesn't matter, there are other universes. Eternity never ends. It is the process that is meaningful because it allows us to savor the experience and express ourselves ... and learn.

Some souls reach the nursery but are unable to handle learning "to be" on an individual basis during early maturation. Later, they are associated with collective functions and never leave the spirit world.

There are energy fragments that have individual soul essences that are not inclined or have the necessary mental fabric to incarnate in physical form on any world. They are often found in mental worlds, and they also appear to move easily between dimensions.

There are energy fragments with individual soul essences that incarnate only in physical worlds. These souls may well receive training in the spirit world with mental spheres between lives, but they are probably not interdimensional travelers.

There are also energy fragments which are souls with the ability and inclination to incarnate and function as individuals in all types of physical and mental environments. This does not necessarily give them more or less enlightenment than other soul types. However, their wide range of practical experience positions them for many specialization opportunities and assignments of responsibility.

Once they leave the nursery, new souls are separated into individual cluster groups at their level of understanding. And, once formed, no new souls are added in the future. There is a systematic selection procedure for homogeneous groupings of souls. Similarities of ego, cognitive awareness, expression, and desire are all considerations. Cluster groups do not intermix with each other's energy, but they can communicate. In Levels I and II, cluster groups can split into smaller study groups but are never separated from their cluster. Some souls advance faster than others, and when a soul shows special talents (e.g., teaching, healing, creating, etc.), they can participate in more advanced work in their specialty while still remaining in their cluster. When a soul enters Level III, they are then formed into independent studies work groups from many clusters within one or more secondary groups. When they approach Level IV, they become more independent outside cluster groups; however, intimate contact between the original cluster group is never lost.

We certainly are infinitesimally small. We are, however, most significant as we are individuated manifestations of Loving Consciousness ... the candle having all the characteristics of the sun, and the drop having all the characteristics of the ocean, no matter their size.

Our soul immediately desires our full expression, and we quickly grow into this desire to BE God. However, as God is constantly growing, as God's component manifestations (us souls) gather more understanding and experience, we will never individually catch up to God. **We will always exist ... as long as God ("All-Loving Awareness") keeps accruing new insights and experiences through the experiences each individual soul gains.**

For Dr. Newton, the soul has an absolute purity within matter or outside of matter. Inside of matter (the human body), it is refracted in its expression by matter. I don't think the soul is ever weighed down or deceived, even in the body. The body can be weighed down and deceived. The body has these positive or negative experiences, and they are transferred to the soul for the development of our soul's growth. The continuing challenge for us here is to remember who and what we are – *love* – and to, over time, throw off those DNA dictates to which we all initially succumb throughout lifetimes in favor of acting like who we are: love. This is the process of choice.

Beginner Souls

There are two types of beginner souls: truly young souls and those who have been around a long time but are immature. They are Levels I and II. Almost three-quarters of all the people on Earth are Level I and Level II.

Each century brings improvement in the awareness of all humans.

When a soul is first created, he doesn't know himself/herself as himself/herself (the soul has no sex) until he/she moves into the quiet place with his/her new guide. This quiet place is like a Maternity Ward arranged like a honeycomb. These are spiritual areas of ego creation where raw, undefined energy can be manipulated into a genesis of Self.

Lower-level souls can lead lives that have many positive elements. Otherwise, no one would advance. *It is impossible to tell what level we are while here on this planet.* There is, and should be, no embarrassment about being a lower-level soul. We all progress by degrees in a complex matter through a variety of ways in an uneven manner. The important thing is to recognize our faults, avoid self-denial, and have the courage and self-sufficiency to make constant adjustments in our lives.

For the younger souls, the first realization that they are part of a substantial group of spirits like themselves is a source of delight. This usually takes place by the end of a fifth life on Earth. Cluster groups are carefully designed to give peer support through a sensitivity of identity traits between all members. This cohesiveness is far beyond what we know on Earth.

Since the complete truth about each other is known by all group members in a telepathic world, humor is indispensable. Some may find it hard to accept that souls do joke with each other about their failings, but humor is the basis upon which self-deception and hypocrisy are exposed.

Ego defenses are so well understood by everyone in spiritual groups that evidence of a mastery of oneself among peers is a strong incentive for change. Spiritual "therapy" occurs because of honest peer feedback, mutual trust, and the desire to advance with others over eons of time. Souls can hurt, and they need caring entities around them. The curative power of spiritual group interaction is quite remarkable.

Spiritual groups are a primary means of soul instruction. Learning appears to come as much from one's peers as from the skill of guides who monitor these groups. However, people tend to think of souls in a free state as being without human deficiencies. There are many similarities between groups of souls close to each other and human family systems.

There is no hatred, suspicion, or disrespect in soul groups. In a climate of compassion, there are no power struggles for control among these peer groups whose members are unable to manipulate each other or keep secrets. Souls distrust themselves, not each other. There is fortitude, desire, and the will to keep trying in their new physical lives.

They are also brought into harmony with each other by means of a cylindrical "cone," small at the top and wide at the bottom, fitting over all of them like a great white cap in which they float. The top funnels energy down as a waterfall, allowing them to concentrate on their mental sameness. It is the Planners, above guides, who probably bring groups together. Individuals in a group have different talents, and they all contribute to the group. A group has marked similarities in talent and interests, but they do have wide variations in expression. Shortcomings and faults are recognized far more in the spirit world than on Earth. In the spirit world, individual ego-identity is constantly enhanced by warm peer group socialization.

Souls also spend time alone in personal reflection when attached to a group. When alone, they spend time concentrating on loved ones on Earth with whom they are close. They go to a "place of projection" where they enter an "interdimensional field of floating, silvery-blue energy" before projecting outward to a geographical area of their choosing. Here, souls ride on their thought waves to specific people, buildings, or a given area of land in an attempt to comfort themselves of change.

To note, without addressing and overcoming pain, you can never really connect with who you are and build on that. The more pain and adversity that comes to you as a child and throughout life, the more opportunity you have to expand your potential.

Intermediate Souls

Souls evolving into the middle development levels have less association with their group because they have acquired the maturity and experience to act more independently. Some also begin to serve as guides, but not all are suited for such a role. Those who have reached the intermediate levels are modest about their achievements, and they possess a remarkable comprehension of a universal life plan. It is not an absolute prerequisite that souls have hundreds of physical lives to advance. Some advance after only 4,000 years, an outstanding performance.

We can live two parallel lives at one time. Very rarely, it can also be three or four because there is no time in the spiritual world. Most souls are better off living one life at a time. The reward for bunching lives together is that it allows more reflection out of incarnation. Since we originate within the Maker, part of our soul remains in the spirit world at all times even when we have two simultaneous incarnations. The part of us that remains in the spirit world when we incarnate remains dormant, waiting to be rejoined to the rest of our energy. When our soul "divides," every part of us is whole.

The Space of Transformation

Because the spirit world does not equate to Earth, the terms used do not often compute. There is a place called the "Rooms of Recreation." We think what we want, and it happens. We are being assisted in what we do there, creating anything familiar to our past experiences.

Souls can become rocks to capture the essence of density, trees for serenity, water for flowing cohesiveness, butterflies for freedom, and beauty and whales for power and immensity. These experiences have nothing to do with former earthly transmigrations. Souls may also become amorphous without substance or texture. They would totally integrate into a particular feeling such as compassion to sharpen their intensity.

Some subjects tell of being mystical spirits of nature such as elves, giants, or mermaids. Personal contacts with strange mythological beasts are mentioned as well. These are all vivid accounts. Are these shared soul experiences? Maybe many of our legends are sympathetic memories of souls carried from other places to Earth long ago.

Spiritual Learning Centers

Any gathering of souls outside a classroom setting, including the large assembly halls, indicates that it is a time of general socializing and recreation. This doesn't mean serious discussions are not taking place in these areas, only that soul activities are not as directed as in study areas. There are also independent study programs.

The teachers of first-level souls do get tired of certain students who almost refuse to progress, so they leave them alone a lot. Teachers have infinite patience because time is meaningless in the spirit world. They are content to wait until the student is disgusted with treading water and offers to work harder.

It is a standard learning imperative that we begin to study our past lives in depth right away. The people who describe earthly structures in their spiritual home also include the library, and descriptions of this setting are quite consistent. On Earth, a library represents a systematic collection of books arranged by subjects and names which provide information. The titles of spiritual life books have individual names on them. These records give the illusion of books with pages, but they are instead sheets of energy that vibrate and form live picture patterns of events. (If someone from Planet X had never been to Earth and whose place of study was an ocean tide pool, that is what this entity would report seeing in the spirit world.)

Eastern philosophy holds that every thought, word, and deed from every lifetime in our past along with every event in which we participated is recorded in the Akashic Record. Possibilities of future events can also be seen with the help of scribes. The word "Akasha" essentially means the essence of all universal memory that is recording every energy vibration of existence. It's like an audio/visual magnetic tape. It's a human conceptualization of spiritual libraries. They are timeless places where we can study missed opportunities and our accountability for past actions. Those are examples of those divine, immortal, and conscious memory connections. People of the East have conceived that the substance of all events past, present, and future are preserved by containment within energy particles before being recovered in a sacred spiritual setting through vibrational alignments. Most probably, the whole concept of personal spiritual records for each of us did not originate in India or anywhere else on Earth. It began with our spiritual minds already having knowledge of these records between lives.

The pictures of spiritual learning environments can change rapidly in the minds of those discussing their instruction periods. Spiritual learning centers are not necessarily visualized as having a classroom or library atmosphere. They are often the "space of our home." The functional aspects of acquiring spiritual knowledge are translated by the human mind into learning centers. Guides have a hand in creating visualizations of earthly edifices for souls who come to our planet.

There is overwhelming kindness, benevolence, and infinite patience for everyone in ethereal study areas. Even the analysis of each soul's performance by fellow students is conducted with total love, respect, and a mutual commitment to make things better in the next incarnation.

Souls love to tease and use humor in their groups, but they always show respect for one another, even with those who have been in bodies that have hurt them in life. More than forgiveness, souls exercise tolerance. They know that most negative personality traits are connected to the ego of the body and the person who brought them sadness and heartache was buried when that body died. At the top of the discarded list of negative emotions are anger and fear.

Souls are not forced to study, and some take long periods of rest. Even so, most souls feel left out if they are not with their classmates on some ongoing project. It is the excitement of mastering certain skills that drives them. Thus, most souls don't wish to get involved in the middle of projects by other groups.

Unlike human beings, all spiritual beings are bonded together. At the same time, souls strictly observe the sanctity of other groups.

An axiom of the spirit world is that souls are always hardest on themselves in terms of performance. Within soul study groups, there is a wondrous clarity of rational thought. Self-delusion does not exist, but the motivation to work hard in every life is not uniform among all souls. Some say, "I'm going to skate for a while." With that, they are going to slow down their rate of incarnations, pick easy incarnations, or both. Although the soul's teachers and council may not be happy with this decision, it is respected. Even within the spirit world, some students choose not to give their best at all times, though they are a distinct minority of earthbound souls.

To the Greeks, the word "persona" was synonymous with "mask." This is an appropriate term for how the soul utilizes a host body for any life. When we reincarnate into a new body, the soul's character is united with the temperament of its host to form one persona. The body is the outward manifestation of the soul, but it is not the total embodiment of our soul Self. Souls who come to Earth think of themselves as becoming masked actors on a stage.

However, these stage analogies by soul groups do not trivialize what they go through on Earth as simple impersonations. They offer the soul an objective means of comprehension and foster a desire to improve. The system is ingenious. *Souls never seem to get bored* in these educational exercises which invite creativity, originality, and a desire to triumph over adversity by acquiring wisdom from human relationships. They always want to do better next time. Whatever the format, spaces of learning provide a fascinating chessboard for souls when they go over all the possible moves for the best solutions after the game is over. Like champion athletes, they want to improve with each performance.

Instruction in learning centers is also not limited to reviewing past lives. Besides all the other activities, energy manipulation is a major part of training. The acquisition of these skills takes many forms in classroom work. Again, humor is a hallmark of the spirit world.

Soul Specializations

There are several soul specializations among the many: **Dreammasters**, **Redeemers of Lost Souls**, **Keepers of Neutrality**, **Restoration Masters**, **Nursery Ethicists**, **Incubator Mothers**, **Archivist Souls**, **Animal Caretaker Souls**, **Musical Directors**, and **Gamekeepers**. While **teaching** is a leading specialty in the spirit world, this does not mean that most souls make great teachers.

Additionally, **Harmonizer Souls** are people like statesmen, prophets, inspirational messengers, negotiators, artists, musicians, and writers. When one becomes proficient at being a Harmonizer, he whispers through the corridors of Earth of better things to come such as messengers of hope and superior beings who care enough about the survival of souls on Earth to watch over us.

Masters of Design can be trainees assigned to work in a physical universe that frequently has uninhabited planets in the process of cooling after being formed out of stars. They are involved with the creation of life forms and are engaged with worlds where new life is evolving, thus having an enormous influence on creation. Master Designers who work with living organisms like biologists or botanists of the spirit world may also say that *extraterrestrial life exists on billions of planets.*

Souls worth noting in a little more depth are **Explorers**. These are souls who experience different environments outside the spirit world between lives, souls whose personal development requires in-depth experience in different worlds, or they can be simply recreational travelers. Most of the souls who explore other worlds are led by instructors. There are physical worlds of fire, water, ice, or gas where all manner of intelligent life thrives. Soul travel often involves working vacations. These visits are usually to physical worlds for souls from Earth and can last from a few days up to hundreds of years in Earth time. Subjects have great empathy for the unspoiled planets which are similar to Earth but with no people. They look upon these places as their own special playgrounds. There are not many of Dr. Newton's subjects with memories of going to mental worlds.

Going through other dimensions is like going through soft, translucent filaments of light. Coming into this universe is like plowing through thick, heavy, moisture-laden fog. Being in this world for the first time is like having concrete tied to your feet. The most troubling aspect of the human brain is impulsive behavior, the physical reaction to things without analytical thought. There is also danger in connecting with the wrong kind of human being: treachery. Earth is considered a dimension with a strenuous physical world that has a reputation for producing vigorous, insightful souls once you survive the lessons. Finishing one's work on Earth produces a strengthening in ways that friends who refused such assignments would not be strengthened.

Various universes are other dimensions of existence. Passing through these dimensions, the first dimension is a sphere full of colors and violent explosions of light, with sound and energy still forming. The next is black and empty, the unused sphere. Then, there is a beautiful dimension that has both physical and mental worlds composed of gentle emotion, tender elements, and keen thought. This dimension is superior to many other dimensions.

Everything is a circle around the center of the spirit world. Each of these universes appears to be an interlocking sphere with the next, like a chain.

Training to be an Explorer soul involves learning about the texture of intelligent energy. (There was not enough that Dr. Newton could learn about the properties of energy in motion on mental worlds.)

Souls who travel inter-dimensionally explain that their movements appear to be in and out of curved spheres connected by zones that are opened and closed by converging vibrational attunement. Explorer trainees have to learn this skill. Interdimensional travelers must also learn about the surface of boundaries of zones connecting universes like hikers locating trailheads between mountain ranges. Souls speak of points, lines, and surfaces in multi-space, which indicate larger structural solids, at least for the physical universes. Dimensions having geometric designs probably need hyperspace to hold them. Yet, Explorer souls travel so fast in some sort of hyperspace that it seems the essence of speed, time, and direction of travel are hardly definitive. Training to be an Explorer must indeed be formidable.

One final soul specialty should be noted: **Timemasters**. These are souls who are coordinators engaged with the past, present, and future timelines of people and events. Timemasters are the highly adroit experts who give the impression of actually directing the presentations in our theater-in-the-round for life selections. These master souls are members of an entire fellowship of planners that includes guides, Archivists, and council Elders who are involved with designing our future.

As they view specific scenes of what the Timemasters want them to see, some souls feel they are playing a chess game where they don't yet know all the possible moves available for a desired ending. Usually, souls look at parts of a future life on a baseline, or **Ring Line** as some subjects call it. The Ring Line represents the greatest probable course of a life for each body examined. The soul preparing for incarnation knows that one chess move, one minute change in the game they are watching, could alter the outcome. It is intriguing that most of the time, souls are not shown any in-depth probable future outcomes. They know there are many other possible moves on the chessboard of life that can change at any moment of play. Frankly, this is what makes the game interesting for most souls. Changes in life are conditional on our free will toward a certain action. This causality is part of the laws of karma. Karma is an opportunity, but it also involves fortitude and endurance because the game will bring setbacks and losses along with personal victories.

Time training is conducted at a temple called the **Temple of Time**, where teachers instruct in the application of energy sequences for events. Timelines exist as energy sequences of events that move. Time is manipulated by the compressing and stretching of energy particles within a unified field to regulate its flow like playing with rubber bands. Energy is the carrier of thought and memory within the sequences, and these never pass into oblivion. The conduit by which time is perceived begins with a thought – the shaping of an idea – then the event and finally the memory of the event. The particles of energy, which are part of the causation for setting up events in time, involve vibrational patterns with many alternatives. All this human history is useful for future incarnations of people.

Souls are capable of going to other universes that have held mightier civilizations than we have on Earth. They could catch glimpses of their conversation, their victories, and the ultimate decisions that caused their demise. We are even capable of going back to our childhood – not recreating it physically but traveling back to it in time – as ghosts to observe our joys and experiences. This would all take the help of an experienced Time Traveler, and experienced teacher.

Graduation from the Primary Soul Group

There comes a time in a soul's existence when it is ready to move away from its primary soul group. It could have taken 1,000 years to finally maintain a soul's identity in each life ... under adverse circumstances, and to honor itself as a human being who could not be superseded by others. This is generally a transition to Level III.

The integrity of a soul's original cluster group remains intact in a timeless way. Regardless of who is graduating, they never lose their bond to their old companions. Primary cluster groups began their existence together and will remain closely associated through hundreds of incarnations into the future. Dr. Newton has had subject souls who were with their primary groups for some 50,000 years before they were ready to move on to the intermediate levels. Meanwhile, a much smaller percentage have achieved this state of development within 5,000 years. Once reaching Level III, souls begin to rise much more rapidly into the advanced levels.

With the attaining of Level III, there is a change in soul behavior. These souls have now begun to expand their vistas away from their primary groups. The advancing souls don't disregard all they have known before, it's just that they are now so engrossed in their training that it has become an all-consuming goal. These souls are fascinated by what they can do and want to become even more proficient. By the time they approach a Level IV range of development, the transition is complete.

The transition is a slow one in keeping with the practice of infinite care that is so evident in all spiritual training. The assignments to new specialty groups are formed with other like-minded souls based upon several considerations. The three principal elements that present themselves in these regressions are talent, past performance, and personal desire. The needs of the spirit world might also be another important element, but this was not shown in Dr. Newton's subjects.

The Advanced Soul

These are very scarce. The mark of an advanced spirit is one who has patience with society and shows extraordinary coping skills. The most prominent sign is exceptional insight. Life still has karmic pitfalls for them, or else they would not be here. They are usually found in the helping professions or combating social injustice. The advanced soul radiates composure, kindness, and understanding toward others.

Souls have probably only been on Earth for a couple of hundred thousand years. Souls eventually made us human, not the reverse. When we say "God," we make the Source too human.

The older, advanced souls can recall being in strange, non-human intelligent life forms on other worlds. Their memories are rather fleeting and clouded by the circumstances of these lives, the physical details, and planetary location relative to our universe.

We communicate by absorbing the energy presence of others. As an advanced soul who returns to that place outside this world, he will be alone for a while to sort out any mistakes from his last incarnation before talking to his guide.

"Sages" or "Old Ones" are highly advanced watchers of the Earth who continue to incarnate to keep watch over what is going on. They live in small communities in deserts, mountains, or simple dwellings. And they simply wander about. When you meet one, you feel a special presence, see a power of understanding, and get excellent advice. These Sages are above Level VI. They are very close to the source. They represent the purest of thought, engaging in the planning and arranging of substances. We all aspire to become one of these.

Advanced souls are also usually guides.

Life Selections

When souls get back to the spirit world, they are tired and don't want to think about returning to Earth again. Eventually, the soul would be motivated to start the process of incarnation again. While our spiritual environment is hard to leave, we as souls also remember the physical pleasures of life on Earth with fondness and even nostalgia. When the wounds of a past life heal and when we are again at one with ourselves, we feel the pull of having a physical expression for our identity once more. The soul must now act based on three primary decisions:

1. Am I ready for a new physical life?
2. What specific lessons do I want to undertake to advance my learning and development?
3. Where should I go, and who should I be, for the best opportunity to work on my goals?

When a world dies, those entities with unfinished business move on to another world that has a suitable life form for the kind of work they have been doing previously. As the population on the Earth grows, we reincarnate much more frequently than we did in the past, often several times in one century. The inventory of souls must truly be astronomical.

Souls do have the freedom to choose when, where, and who they want to be in their physical lives. Certain souls spend less time in the spirit world to accelerate development while others are very reluctant to leave. Without life in a physical body, studies would take longer. If you miss out on having direct experience, you will miss a great deal.

Once a soul has decided to incarnate again, the next stage in the return process is to be directed to the place of life selection, a screening room of future lives called the **Ring of Destiny**. This is where we first behold our next body. Souls consider when and where they want to go before deciding on who they will be in their lives.

Most subjects use similar language to describe their life selection. They are said to resemble a movie theater which allows souls to see themselves in the future playing different roles in various settings. Before leaving, souls will have selected one scenario for themselves. A "dress rehearsal" before the performance of a new life then starts!

We preview our new life in the Ring, a monster bubble of concentrated energy force and an intense light whose energy relaxes us. Our trainer is also there with us. The Ring is surrounded by a bank of scenes, like mirrors, that one can look at. It is quiet at first, and then the whole panorama begins to move and come alive with images, color, action, and sound. There is a control panel in front like the cockpit of a plane. I help the controllers change the images on the screen with my mind as I travel through time with them through the screens. I don't control the scenes of life, but I do control my movement through them like a video with stop, start, fast forward, and reverse. I can experience what life is like on the screen or watch it from any vantage point. We don't disturb the life cycles when traveling through time. We test our ability to find solutions, and we gauge our abilities against the difficulty of the events. The Ring sets up different experiments to choose from. But we can't frolic here because there are serious decisions to be made for the next life. I'll have to accept the consequences of my mistakes in my choices, especially if I am not able to handle a life well.

The purpose of reincarnation is the exercise of free will. Whatever happens to us in life, our happiness or pain does not reflect blessings or betrayal by God-oversoul, our guides, or our life coordinators. *We are the masters of our destiny.*

When I am done in the Ring, I have mostly made up my mind about the specifics of my next life. I then go back and talk to my companions before making up my mind completely.

According to the experiences of Dr. Newton's subjects, the souls of young children who die soon after birth will return to the same parents as the soul of their next baby. These plans are all made in advance by the souls of those participating in tragic family events. Souls essentially volunteer in advance for bodies that will have sudden fatal illnesses, will be killed by someone, or will end abruptly with many others from a catastrophic event.

Aside from all other considerations, incarnation comes down to souls making that all-important decision for a specific body, and what can be learned by utilizing the brain of a certain human being.

People have the idea that **free will** and **destiny** are opposing forces. They do not realize that destiny represents the sum of our deeds over thousands of years in a multitude of incarnations. In all these lives, we had freedom of choice. Thousands, millions of free choice decisions rolling down over many lives throughout eternity create our destiny. Our current lives represent all past experiences both pleasant and unpleasant. So, we are the product of all our former choices. Add to this the fact that we may have deliberately placed ourselves in situations that test how we will react to events in our current life, which are not perceived by the conscious mind. This too involves personal choices. We occupy a particular body for many reasons.

Earth is considered by souls to be a very difficult school. The great lesson of Earth is to overcome both planetary and private destructive forces in life, grow strong from the effort, and move on from it all.

To a great extent, we come equipped with what we need to take care of ourselves. Karma may at times seem punitive, but there is justice and balance that we may not recognize in our sorrow. Fear arises when we separate ourselves from our spiritual power. We know many of the challenges in advance of our lives, and we choose them for good reasons. Accidents involving our bodies are not considered to be accidental by the soul.

The sheer will of our true Self has the power to rise in opposition to our weakness in character, especially during adversity. We have the freedom to remake our lives after any catastrophe if we are willing to take the responsibility to do so. More important than the events that test us is our reaction to these events and how we handle the consequences.

Choosing a New Body

In our place of life selection, our souls preview the life span of more than one human being within the same time cycle. Our spiritual advisors give us ample time to reflect on the life we will choose. Great care must be taken in choosing just the right body for our next lifetime. Guides and peer group members would help us in our choice. Often, a person who has skated through one life would overwhelm himself in the next lifetime to catch up with their learning process. Regardless of our soul level, being human means that we will make mistakes and must make mid-course corrections in response.

Even though we know in advance what we are going to look like in our next life, 90% of both males and females would be dissatisfied with the physical characteristics of their earthly bodies. Many handicapped people feel they were the product of a genetic mistake or an accident, whereas there are few accidents that don't fall under the free will of souls. It is difficult to tell someone who was just injured that he still has the opportunity to advance at a faster rate than those with healthy bodies. We can get stronger with adversity.

The real lessons of life are learned by recognizing and coming to terms with being human. Even as victims, we are beneficiaries. It is how we stand up to failure and duress that really marks our progress in life. Sometimes, one of the most important lessons is to learn to just let go of the past.

While souls carefully consider the physical attributes of an Earth body in a variety of cultural settings, they give much more attention to the psychological aspects of human life. This decision is the most vital part of the entire selection process for the soul. Before entering the place of Life Selection, it is to a soul's advantage to ponder the factors of heredity and environment which affect how a biological life form will function. Souls who unite with people who develop early personality disorders deliberately set themselves up for a difficult life.

Human beings without souls would be dominated by senses and emotions. The soul does not control the human mind. It tries by its presence to elevate it, see its meaning in the world, be receptive to morality, and give understanding.

The hard tasks we set for ourselves often begin in childhood. The idea that each of us voluntarily agreed to be the children of a given set of parents before we came into this life is a difficult concept for some people to accept. To know ourselves spiritually means understanding why we joined with the souls of parents, siblings, spouses, and close friends. There is usually some karmic purpose for receiving pain or pleasure from someone close to us. Remember, along with learning our own lessons, we come to Earth to play a part in the drama of others' lessons as well. It is the ultimate in compassion when beings who are spiritually linked to each other come forward by prior agreement into human lives involving love-hate relationships. Overcoming adversity in these relationships may mean we won't have to repeat certain abrasive alliances in future lives again.

If the human personality has little structure beyond the five senses and basic drives for survival without ensoulment, then **the soul IS our total personality**. This means, for example, that one can have a human ego that is jealous and also possess a soul that is not jealous.

We may express ourselves differently with each body. Souls apparently select bodies that try to match their character flaws with human temperament for specific growth patterns. We don't need to change who we are in relation to life's experiences, only our negative reactions to these events need focus. Asian Buddhists say enlightenment is seeing the absolute soul ego reflected in the relative human ego and acting through it during life.

In extreme cases, a fractured personality struggling with internalized conflicts may result in a dissociative reaction to reality. Dr. Newton feels that this is a sign the soul is not always able to regulate and unify with the human mind. If we become obsessed with our physical bodies or get carried along on an emotional roller coaster in life, the soul can be subverted by its outer self. Many great thinkers in history believed that the soul can never be fully homogeneous with the human body, and that humans have two intellects. Dr. Newton considers human ideas and imagination as emanating from the soul, which provides a catalyst for the human brain. How much reasoning power we would have without souls is impossible to know. But apparently, the attachment of souls to humans supplies us with insight and abstract thought. The soul offers humans a qualitative reality subject to conditions of heredity and environment.

There is no more correlation with advanced souls being drawn to human brains with high intelligence than there is with immature souls being drawn to bodies with lower intellectual aptitudes.

Regardless of body choice, souls do demonstrate their individualism through the human mind. A person may be highly intelligent and yet have a closed attitude about adjusting to new situations with little curiosity about the world. This indicates a beginner soul. If someone with an evenness of mood has interests and abilities solidly in focus and directed toward helping human progress, that is probably an advanced soul at work. It does seem like a heavy burden that in every new life, a soul must search all over again to find its true self in a different body. Some light is allowed through the blackout of amnesia by spiritual masters who are not indifferent to our plight. When it comes to finding soulmates on Earth and remembering aspects of the lives we saw in the place of life selection, there is an ingenious form of coaching that is given to souls just before the next life.

There are **life-selection rooms** in which the soul planning a new life sees sheets of film that look like waterfalls that can be entered while part of our energy stays in the room. All cosmic viewing screens are multidimensional with coordinates to record spacetime avenues of occurrence. These are often referred to as timelines, and they can be manipulated by thought scanning. There may be other directors of this process not seen by the soul. Quite often, a subject will employ mechanical contrivances scanning descriptions such as panels, levers, and dials. Apparently, these are all illusions created for souls who incarnate on Earth. Souls would take a portion of their energy, leaving the rest at the console, to enter the screens in one of two ways. They can either be like ghosts who take no part in the events in a virtual reality-like situation, or they will assume roles in the action of the scene even to the extent of altering reality from the original through recreating the events.

We practice interactions with those we love and with whom we choose to come to Earth with over and over again. This is so that we won't dance by them and miss one of the main purposes that we would have chosen a particular life. We practice our future meeting with that person so that we will then say, "Wait a minute!" and engage with that person. This will allow for what we came for to fall into place.

The conscious mind may or may not be able to translate into human language what the superconscious mind fully sees in the library.

Preparation for Embarkation/the Place of Recognition

One might think that once souls have a new body choice as well as the physical and psychological attributes selected, they would incarnate directly to Earth. However, this doesn't happen until a significant element of preparation occurs. We must prepare ourselves to find the souls who will be important to us, and also find those with whom we will play an important role. So, we go to the Place of Recognition, and – in effect – cram as if for a final exam.

For most of us, the soul closest to us on Earth is our spouse. But they could be other family members or a close friend as well. The amount of time they spend with us can be long or short. What matters is the impact they have on us while here.

Connecting with beings we know from the spirit world, in all sorts of physical disguises, can be harmonious or frustrating. *The lesson we must learn from human relationships is accepting people for who they are without expecting our happiness to be dependent upon anyone.*

There are no happenstances, spontaneous or impulse meetings of souls who are crucial contacts. They are all preplanned. This makes them no less romantic. It is also true that our conscious amnesia can make meeting significant people difficult, and we may take a wrong turn and miss the connection at some juncture.

So, we have recognition classes to not miss other important souls while on Earth. We interact and learn to recognize the 10 to 15 people who will be important to us in our life to come. We get prompters (signs placed in our way to jog our memory) so that we will know what to look for in our next life. These are like road signs that kick us into a new direction in life to know what is coming. There is then a final "class review" bringing all of it together. We are brought together to recognize the times in our lives when these people will appear for us to remember some action, the way they look, or something about them. After this class, we usually don't forget the important signs. We would already know most of the souls who will be important to us on Earth. If we don't, we will meet them in class.

Eyes are the windows to our soul, and no other physical attribute is more important when souls meet on Earth. Souls also remember sounds and smells. All five senses can be used to recognize the signals in future lives.

We might miss what we have planned, and we have the right to do that. But sometimes, it will just come to you. Don't intellectualize coming events too much. Some of our best decisions come from instinct. Go with gut feelings. When some special moment is meant to happen, it usually does.

Sometimes, souls return to their spirit group to say goodbye. Other times, they leave directly for Earth from the Place of Recognition.

Rebirth

When we have gone through the bath and a counseling session with our guide,

we are then ready for an orientation with a panel of superior beings, three to seven beings on a Council of Elders. Every Council of Elders is different for every human being.

Here again, we are confronted with our human way of looking at things. Although this Council of Elders is there to go through our life with us, there is no condemnation, only overwhelming understanding. For those things we messed up, we will be given another lifetime to clear them up. These elders or great spiritual advisors are not there to humiliate us. Rather, they are there to greet us with warmth and love. We will face up to what we did again and again when we get back to the other side, but never because of a difficult look or an angry voice from the Council of Elders.

Before we get to the area where we are to meet this council, we gather in a giant staging area. Here, souls are gathered, organized, and sent out to various parts of the universe. There is no confusion or hesitation in this phase.

And there is also no apprehension about destiny. We are thrilled to be with such an august group. The universe has become much more defined now than it was when we first got here with individuals appearing like bright stars. We are literally engulfed in anticipation of our welcome by the elders. And then, there we are, pulled along in a sort of river that gets larger with massive numbers of people floating along until we get pulled into tributary-like slower flows that have fewer people. It is the higher spirits who control who goes where, and it is all done with a kind of loving acceptance. Once again, there is no hesitation in our going. Along the way, we seem to assemble in a cluster where we know everyone. We are among friends. We are thrilled to be going where we seem to be. It is a great honor. And then, we are home, where our friends are. No one is a stranger here. We recognize the universal bond that unites all people; there is no suspicion. There is a total lack of hostility.

Earth has left us with the remnants of fear and violence. We gradually will lose that as we stay here. There is no fear or violence in this place where peace and excitement about life and its forward-looking thrust prevail.

My particular Council of Elders gathers me in and begins a soft line of questioning. Unlike a judge's questioning of a prisoner, the line of inquiry may be direct. But there is a faint wisp of a smile on the elders' faces. Their questions are direct and pull no punches, but they are never made to embarrass. There is also no fear of this process, for we will have learned by now that there is no fear here.

Sometimes, especially for the younger souls, the questioning gets hard to answer and hard to understand. That is when the guide steps in to interpret for us. The longer we have been around, the better we get at this.

Rebirth is a profound experience. Before leaving, it is the last chance for souls to enjoy the omniscience of knowing just who they are before they must adapt to a new body. Most souls have mixed emotions about leaving, but everyone wishes the departing soul well.

The soul begins to move at a greater speed. Then, the soul is aware of its guide leaving. He is alone passing through folds of silky cloth at a smoother and faster rate. Everything becomes blurred as the soul begins sliding down a long, dark tube with a hollow feeling, darkness ... then warmth. We are now inside our mother, and we are a baby.

The soul and the body are two distinct entities at pre-birth. It takes them until about year six in human life to become compatibly merged. At death, they will separate again. The body recognizes the soul as its friend and helper.

The Eastern teaching that nirvana will be the end of each of us when we achieve it would probably be true if Divinity were static and not growing as Divinity's manifestations were growing. As Buddha says, if we ever achieved this nirvana (but over many more lifetimes than Buddha ever probably imagined), then we would in fact dissipate, evaporate, or cease to be. But if God is a growing reality of all of God's manifestations, we will NEVER catch up and always exist because we are always trying to get *there*.

When your soul joins with (your) baby, it should be like placing your hand into a glove that is the exact size for you and the child. Sometimes, however, they don't fit too well.

This is a more rapid transition than the way back. As souls who enter babies, we come from a state of all-knowing. Thus, we are mentally able to adjust more quickly to our surroundings than at the end of a physical life. We are also given additional time for adaptation while we are in the mother's womb. *The physical shock of birth is much greater than the physical shock of death.*

At some point before birth, the soul will carefully touch and join more fully with the impressionable, developing brain of the baby. When a soul decides to enter a baby, that child apparently has no free choice in accepting or rejecting the soul. At the moment of the first entry, chronological time begins for the soul. Depending upon the inclinations of the particular soul involved, the connection may be early or late in the mother's pregnancy. Occasionally, souls time their arrival at the last minute during delivery, but this is unusual. Those souls who join the baby early seem to do a lot of traveling outside the mother's womb during her term.

Once birth has taken place, the union of spirit and flesh would be fully solidified into a partnership. The immortal soul then becomes the seat of perception for developing the human ego. *The soul brings a spiritual force which is the heritage of infinite consciousness.* Although Dr. Newton has said that souls can be confined by a human in trauma, they are never trapped. *Besides leaving at the moment of death, souls may also come and go when the body is sleeping, in deep meditation, or under an anesthetic in surgery.* The soul's absences are much longer in cases of severe brain damage and coma. Some souls float around more than others, going in and out of the baby until birth because they get bored. Other souls goof off and play when the baby is less active. They bounce around the Earth to visit each other and go to interesting places where they once lived in their former lives.

The soul knows whether or not the baby is going to come to full term, be aborted, or die. There is no surprise for the soul. It may be around just to comfort the child. There was never a full life assignment to an aborted baby as far as the child was concerned. The ones who die very early in the womb do not need a soul.

Souls join to their assigned hosts in the womb of the baby's mother sometime after the third month of pregnancy so that they will have a sufficiently evolved brain to work with before term. As part of the fetal state, they are still able to think as immortal souls while they get used to brain circuitry and the alter ego of their host. *After birth, an amnesiac memory block sets in and souls meld their immortal character with the temporary human mind to produce a combination of traits for a new personality.* **In other words, the soul does not FULLY join to the baby's physical body until birth.** (Readers, please remember this when discussing or arguing the dispute on abortion.)

Once the soul attaches to a child, it is necessary to bring its mind into synchronization with the brain. They have to get used to each other. The soul is in the mind of the child, but separate. They have to get used to each other, so the soul goes slowly at first. There is no forcing, and tracing is done carefully. The soul disrupts nothing while it learns the brain wave patterns of the baby such as how this child translates signals and its capacity. No two children are the same. There is a melding. There is an emptiness before the soul's arrival, which the soul fills to make the baby whole. The soul expands the baby's intellect and brings a comprehension of things, a recognition of the truth of what the brain sees. The soul unifies an undeveloped mind. She recognizes the soul as a friend who is going to be part of her. It's as if the baby was waiting for the soul to come. Perhaps, a higher power prepares the baby for the soul.

Unification is not completed by birth, but they have now started to complement each other. The soul stops leaving the child at about five or six years of age and gets fully operational when the child starts school.

Inside the mother's womb is a warm comfortable feeling of love. (Only sometimes stress.) This time is used to think and plan what the soul is going to do after birth. The soul thinks of past lives and missed opportunities, and gains incentive to act on them.

The energy of the soul can be divided into identical parts, similar to a hologram. It may live parallel lives in other bodies, although this is much less common than we sometimes read about. However, because of the dual capability of all souls, part of our light energy always remains behind in the spirit world. Thus, it is possible to see your mother upon returning from a life even though she may have died 30 Earth years before and reincarnated again.

Science tells us that there is NOTHING that happens without a physical trigger causing it. If we stopped there, humanity could logically conclude that a god does not exist because life itself is determinative and not individual choices. But looking back even further to before we were born in each lifetime, we know that each Life Force ("soul") CHOOSES its experiences before arrival, but it does not make the choices themselves. We set ourselves up for the physical stimuli that cause the experience and memory (Which comes first, the chicken or the egg?)

Joining of Soul and Body

There is a kind of ego relegated to the brain which experiences the external world through the senses governing action and reaction. It is this functional organism – created before the soul arrives – that the soul must join. The soul and brain of a new baby appear to begin their association as two separate and distinct entities before becoming one mind. Some people are bothered that the two-entity position, or duality of body and spirit, means that while the immortal character of the soul lives on, the temporary personality of the body dies. Yet, it is the soul in concert with the mind of a body that creates a unique personality of a single Self. Although the physical organism of the body will die, the soul who occupied that body never forgets the host which allowed it to experience Earth in a particular time and place.

When a soul reaches Level III, most can make rapid adjustments once inside a fetus.

Certain body matches do produce lives of frustration and very difficult challenges. However, only two clients of Dr. Newton had a soul who admitted that they asked to be replaced in a fetus they found impossible to adjust to in any way. In both cases, another soul took its place before the eighth month. A prenatal exchange due to incompatibility is an extremely rare occurrence because this is what the life selection room is all about. *This is a factor that can also have some bearing on the discussion about the morality and effect of conscious abortion, that the soul can occasionally change in an individual fetus.*

The soul views the human body as a gift. One said, "This is such a multifaceted planet. Sure, this place brings heartache, but it is delightful too, and incredibly beautiful. The human body is a marvel of form and structure. I never cease to be awed by each new body, the many different ways I can express myself in them, especially in the most important way – love."

With the continued evolution and the influence of souls as a stimulus, some souls forecast the future of human babies as having **mental telepathy**, which is the way souls communicate.

Soul Division and Reunification

The capacity for souls to divide their energy essence influences many aspects of soul life. Perhaps, soul extension would be a more accurate term than soul division. *All souls who come to Earth leave a part of their energy behind in the spirit world*, even those living parallel lives in more than one body. The percentages of energy that souls leave behind may vary, but each particle of light is an exact duplicate of every other Self and replicates the whole identity. This phenomenon is analogous to the way light images are split and duplicated in a hologram. If only a small percentage of a soul's energy is left behind in the spirit world, that particle of Self is more dormant because it is less concentrated. However, because this energy remains in a pure, uncontaminated state, it is still potent.

The ability of a soul to unite with itself is a natural process of energy regeneration after physical death. If we were to bring 100% of our energy into one body during an incarnation, we would blow the circuits of the brain. A full charge of all a soul's energy into one human body would totally subjugate the brain to the soul's power. This could happen with even the less potent, undeveloped souls.

When you are not in harmony with a body, it takes more personal soul energy. If your environment is harsh, that too must be taken into consideration. There are many variables and that is the challenge. That's what is fun.

Having all the soul's energy capacity in one body would negate the whole process of growth for the soul on Earth because it would have no challenge coping with the brain. By strengthening a variety of parts in a soul's total energy through different incarnations, the whole is made stronger. Full awareness at 100% would have another adverse effect. If we did not divide our energy, we would experience a higher level of spiritual memory retention in each human body. Amnesia forces us to go into the testing area of the laboratory of Earth without the answers for the tasks we were sent here to accomplish in the first place.

Amnesia also relieves us of the baggage of past failures so we may use new approaches with more confidence.

It is possible for souls to miscalculate the percentage of energy concentration they bring into a life. One client called this "our light quotient." Level IV and V subjects shortchange themselves more than the less developed souls. Typically, a highly advanced soul will bring no more than 25% of its total capacity to Earth whereas the average, less confident soul has 50% to 70%. The energy of more evolved souls is refined, elastic, and vigorous in smaller quantities. This is why the younger soul must bring more energy into their early incarnations.

Every soul has a specific energy field pattern which reflects as an immortal blueprint of its character, regardless of the number of divided parts. When this spiritual ego is combined with a more structured personality of a physical brain, a higher-density field is produced. The subtleties of this symbiosis are so intricate that this analysis only scratches the surface. Both blueprints of energy react to each other in an infinite number of ways to become one to the outside world. This is why our physical well-being, senses, and emotions are so tied to the spiritual mind. Thought is closely associated with how these energy patterns are shaped and melded together, and each nourishes the other in our bodies.

Think of taking a photograph of the same scene in the morning, at noon, and in the evening. The changes in light refraction would create a different effect on the film. The energy of souls begins with a specific pattern. But once on Earth, these patterns are changed by local conditions. When we review our future life from the spirit world, we are given advice about the energy requirements of the body that we will occupy. The decision of how much energy we should take is ours. Many souls want to leave as much behind as possible because they love their home and the activities going on there.

One of the best ways we revitalize our energy is through sleep. Once again, we can further divide the energy we brought with us and roam freely while leaving a small percentage behind to alert the larger portion to return quickly if needed. This capacity is especially useful when the body is in a state of illness, unconsciousness, or in a coma. Since time is not a limiting factor for a freed soul, hours, days, or weeks away from the body are all rejuvenating. Souls can also be recharged by loving spirits during a crisis. We interpret these energy boosts as profound revelations. A few hours' rest from the human body can do wonders for a soul as long as the remaining portion left behind is on cruise control and not coping with a complex dream analysis. That circumstance may cause us to wake up exhausted.

Many people feel it is common for souls to live parallel lives. This is apparently not true at all. The souls who choose to split into two or more bodies within the general time frame on Earth want to accelerate their learning. Thus, a soul might leave up to 10% of its energy behind and place the rest in two or three bodies. Because we have free will, our guides will allow for these experiments, but they do advise against it. On the whole, since the energy drain is enormous, most souls who try parallel lives do so only a time or two before giving it up. Souls don't wish to lead parallel lives unless they are extraordinarily ambitious. Also, souls don't split their energy to incarnate as twins, which would be counterproductive.

Chapter 6
Guides

All our life, we have heard about "guardian angels." It is another term for "guide," one of our most important allies as we attempt to grow from an immature soul to a wise and mature one. "Guardian angel" is just an older, more religious term for the same thing, except that guides have always lived human lives on Earth, and guardian angels were said not to have done so.

Guides mature also. Every individual seems to have one or more guides, with the younger or newer ones training and learning from the more experienced guides. So, we may feel the influence of two or more guides during our earthly visit. They stay with us for thousands of lives on this Earth. And they are constantly guiding us, nudging us, and inspiring us. They can give us a thought or a new angle on life's situations.

Guides are systematically assigned to us with attention given to a guide's proclivity toward our personalities. There is a fine blend, and the guide will exhibit a sense of humor, an ability to let things ride, or any number of ways to display a finely tuned obligation toward inciting us to do well. They never give up on us over hundreds of lives and thousands of years, and they have a fierce loyalty to their charges. Their chief function is to motivate us and instill courage to get through life's challenges. When we stubbornly refuse to face the challenges of life and when we refuse to take the advice of our guides, those guides make themselves scarce. We each send out thin waves subconsciously to the far reaches of the universe, where anyone tuned into our fingerprinted wavelength can get them. When we send an announcement of our predicament, our guide is always there to answer us in the most clarity we can accept. If we are calm and relaxed, we can hear that inner voice. If we are nervous and noisy, if we allow our mind to hammer a hundred things at once into our brains, that nudge from our guide is easily missed. If you want help, ask for the next logical thing to do, the next most loving thing. Do not ask for the ultimate solution. Then the next logical step will be forthcoming. You can hear it if you are at ease and have a clear mind. That is one of the main reasons people meditate.

To reach our spiritual guide, we simply have to call to him. We expand our inner conscience outward to encompass more of life. If we are not calm, we will have a hard time reaching our guide. Being calm is the receptive element that cannot be forgotten. For the guide, this is important as well. She must learn to be attentive and wait for the right moment. A person in trouble or pain sends out many messages, and it can be tiring to listen and respond to everyone with no guarantee the person is listening. A guide has to wait for the emotions to die down.

For example, when a person is in intense grief, that person can rarely be reached. The mind is so cluttered that a guide will simply have to wait until energy is gathered and the mind is quieter.

For those who have had a difficult life filled with traumatic experiences and difficult choices, which they may or may not have handled well, the first person they see after leaving their earthly life is their spiritual guide. They are always there, although they can seem absent sometimes when the soul goes home, but he will see them later. But they will always be there.

Guides are spiritual beings who stay with us throughout our many lives on Earth. Our guide is a very important aspect of our existence, at least through our Earth journeys, which may last thousands of years through hundreds or thousands of lifetimes. It is difficult to describe the degree to which our guides form our lives.

Guides are spiritual teachers who bring people into the company of warm, loving, and creative power. They make us more acutely aware of the continuity of life and our identity as souls. They are figures of grace in our existence because they are part of the fulfillment of our destiny. Guides, especially master guides, are complex entities. Master guides may have a lot of souls on Earth and in the spirit world to look over, but they can handle it. Souls may also have a senior guide and a junior guide (who is assigned to us later in our development).

Junior guides can begin as guides toward the end of Earth Level III. They're assigned to us in an orderly fashion and are matched to our permanent soul identity. They are compassionate because they have been through a lot, without being judgmental. They do not impose their values on souls, but rather motivate and instill courage are you outside. Guides are gentle but probing, and nothing can be hidden from them. The exploration of attitudes and feelings to reorient future behavior is typical of guides. We don't get to choose our guide, he/she chooses us. We never fear our guide, but we do worry whether they will leave us during difficult periods (they won't). We send out constant spiritual fingerprints, which our guide is aware of. We have the feeling that we are being watched over, and they will always answer us (but can *we* hear?). Guides do have the ability to screen their thoughts from souls, especially if their knowledge would confuse the soul.

When we reach Levels III and IV, we are given more responsibility for younger souls. Some begin to train as guides while still returning to Earth for incarnations. But some are not suited to be guides.

One person in 10 admits to hearing voices. These are the voices of our guides. We "see" them in the feelings and emotions that convince us that we are not alone.

When asking for help, open yourself up to the next step and don't reach for the ultimate solution. Do things one step at a time. Go forth in faith and humility that you are moving on the right track. Guides do leave souls alone for long periods of time when they are not needed.

To hear from someone not on Earth – a guide, or really any other related soul – the person on Earth has to first calm their mind and focus attention away from their immediate surroundings. In silence, we reach inward to fasten on our inner voice. We must expand our inner consciousness to engage our guide on a central thought. We must reach out beyond what is troubling us to be receptive to our guide. That is difficult when we are not calm. After that, the guide will whisper in our ears and can merge with our troubled thoughts to calm us. They implant ideas, which we think we think to be *our* inspiration.

Finally, there are also those angel-like spirits who regularly come to Earth between lives simply to help people they don't know who are in distress. Sometimes, they may be healers in training.

Chapter 7
Some Characteristics of Universal Life

Soulmates

The time between the first and second council meetings is a period of renewal for the soul. As ethereal beings, our growth actually began in the mental realm of the spirit world alongside other souls before any of us incarnated. *While our internal being is uniquely individual, a vital part of spiritual life between incarnations is devoted to empathetic relationships with other souls.* Thus, our development as souls becomes a collective one. Part of the expression of this collectivity is the association we have with these souls in a material reality such as Earth. During reincarnation, the closeness souls feel for each other in a mental setting is severely tested by karmic challenges in our host bodies. This interruption of a blissful mental existence is one means by which spiritual masters expand our consciousness.

Love takes hard work and continual maintenance. Dr. Newton had numerous divorced subjects who learned that their first loves were primary soulmates. Things might have worked out if they both had tried harder.

If the right love for you does not come along, liberate yourself with the understanding that you may be here to learn other lessons. We mistakenly assume people who choose to live alone are lonely when actually they have rich lives that are calm, reflective, and productive.

Categories of Soulmates

A principal or primary soulmate is frequently in our life as a closely bonded partner. This partnership may be our spouse, brother, sister, best friend, or occasionally a parent. No other soul is more important to us than a primary soulmate. And when Dr. Newton's subjects describe lives with these souls as their mates, most will say their existence is enriched beyond measure. The advanced soul may change genders from life to life together. The average soul usually chooses one gender over another about 75% of the time.

Our primary soulmate is our eternal partner, but we have other souls in our primary cluster group who can be called soulmates. Essentially, they are our <u>soul companions</u>. These souls have differences in character and a variety of talents which complement each other. Within this cluster group, there is usually an inner circle of souls who are especially close to us. They play important support roles in our lives, and we do the same thing for them. This number varies, but *the average subject has anywhere from three to five souls in their innermost circle*, which is a part of their primary group.

Although the companion souls in a cluster group start together, they do have different rates of development. This has as much to do with drive and motivation as talent. Each soul does possess certain strengths that their companions can draw upon during group incarnations. As the group gets smaller, many go off into different specializations, but they do not lose contact with each other.

<u>Affiliated souls</u> pertain to members of secondary groups outside our primary cluster but are located in the same general spiritual vicinity. *Secondary groups around our primary group can total up to 1,000 souls or more.* There are certain affiliated souls in other groups who are selected to work with us and with whom we would come to know over many lives. Meanwhile, other souls may only cross our path briefly. Surprisingly for most of us, our parents often come from one of these nearby groups and not from our primary group.

In terms of social interaction in the spirit world, as well as contact during their physical incarnations, souls of one cluster group may have little or no association with many of the souls in a secondary group. In the larger context, all souls in a secondary group are affiliated, but they are not considered soulmates by Dr. Newton's subjects. Although they are not companion souls, they do form a large pool of people available for casting calls by our directors in the life to come. A soul affiliate might have a specific characteristic that is exactly what is needed to bring a karmic lesson into your life. They are very likely to incarnate as people who carry strong positive or negative energy into their association with you. These decisions depend upon advance agreements between all parties and their respective teachers with regard to the advantages and disadvantages of certain character roles. The role can be very brief.

Small children who were killed with those who love them will rise with those people. But primary soulmates killed at the same moment will normally rise through separate routes on their own vibrational lines because each soul requires his or her own rate of ascension, which includes orientation stops and energy rejuvenation, even if they are returning to the same soul group.

As a rule, members of the same soul group do not return to their next incarnations as members of the same genetic human family. It is limiting, and even redundant, for souls who wish to learn fresh lessons to return to bodies that have the same heredity, ethnicity, cultural environment, and perhaps the same geographic setting as they had in a former life. By incarnating in different families around the globe for each life, souls can take advantage of the great variety of human body choices. This variety is what gives depth to our incarnations on Earth. Although souls typically do not incarnate in the same hereditary family that they've had in past lives, members of the same soul group most definitely choose new families where they can be together. Members of soul groups tend to be associated with each life by blood ties and geographic proximity.

Grandparents often have a great influence in our early lives as nonjudgmental confidants. A favorite grandparent in this life would often be a sibling or best friend in a former life. Peripheral roles in our lives by hundreds of affiliated souls from nearby groups may go on for generations.

Hybrid Souls

Hybrid souls are especially prone to self-destruction on Earth because they have incarnated on alien worlds fairly recently before coming here. These souls would have great difficulty adapting to our planet. It is probable that their first incarnation here was within the last few thousand years while the others have already adapted or left Earth for good. Less than a quarter of all of Dr. Newton's clients can recall memories of visiting other worlds between lives. This activity by itself does not make them hybrids. An even smaller percentage have memories of actually incarnating on alien worlds before they came to Earth. These are the hybrid souls.

The hybrid is usually an older soul who, for a number of reasons, has decided to complete their physical lives on our planet. Their old world may no longer be habitable, or they may have lived in a gentle world where life was just too easy. Instead, they want a difficult challenge with a world like Earth that has not yet reached its potential. Regardless of the circumstances for a soul choosing to leave a world, these former incarnations typically involve life forms that were slightly above, about equal to, or slightly below the intelligence capabilities of the human brain. This is by design. Many hybrid souls formally incarnated on planets with civilizations possessing a much higher technology level than Earth. Just as those with space travel abilities are smarter because they are an older race, so are hybrid souls with their former experience on a telepathic world allowing them to have greater psychic abilities than normal.

A vast majority of hybrids are fine, and they make great contributions to human society.

Some Souls Can End Their Own Existence

This is important. Many of us have wondered, given the evil of some souls/humans, if a soul could simply disappear, evaporate, or cease to exist. The answer is YES, to a certain extent.

One of the reasons is that there is also a dark side to hybrid souls. They can become atrocity souls, who are associated with acts of evil that are so serious that they are unsalvageable in their present state. They are met by guides and perhaps one close friend before being separated quickly so that the impact of their deeds – the harm and pain they caused on Earth – is not so easily forgotten. Some real monsters on Earth are hybrids. In this place of separation, the souls here are the results of habitually cruel lifestyles. Most will not come back to Earth; they are too fearful that they will fall again into the same patterns. They also lack the courage to be victims in several future lives to work off their karma. These souls will then go the way of *those souls considered to be unsalvageable. Their energy is disseminated.* Dissemination is the breaking up of energy into particles. One particle of old energy might be mixed with nine particles of new energy, providing a freshness like a new start. Even though the souls who accept these procedures for their benefit recover and eventually lead productive lives on Earth and elsewhere, some souls will not stand for any loss of identity. Those souls will go into limbo, a place of solitude. Dr. Newton was unable to find out what eventually happened to those souls.

When we see people who are victims of great adversity in life, this does not necessarily mean they were perpetrators of evil or wrongdoing of any kind in a former life. A soul with no such past associations might choose to suffer through a particular aspect of emotional pain to learn greater compassion and empathy for others by volunteering in advance for a life of travail.

Transformers

Transformers do repair jobs on Earth. They are the clean-up crew in transforming bodies to good health. There are people on Earth who have grey spots of energy, which causes them to get stuck. You see it when they make the same mistakes over and over in life. Transformers incarnate, find those stuck souls, and try to remove these blocks so that they can make better decisions and gain confidence and self-value. They transform souls on Earth to be more productive people. They use a focus beam – like a laser – to pinpoint and clean up this gray energy. This is the fastest way.

There is never an outside force of evil trying to take over a body. However, negative energy blockages in our energy field do cause a reduction in functional capacity.

The secret to healing is removing the conscious self to avoid inhibiting the free flow of energy between the transformer and the person to be healed. The transformer's objective is to merge with the energy flow of the patient to bring out the highest good in that body. This is done with love as well as technique. If the receiving party is resistant and inhibits the free-flowing passageways of chi, or life force, through their mental negativism, they are perfectly capable of blocking the detection of their energy field by a healer.

Souls of Solitude

It is considered a part of normal activity for healthy souls in the spirit world to engage in periods of quiet time away from others. Besides reflecting upon their goals, souls may use this interval to reach out and touch people they left behind on Earth.

Ghosts and Other Souls Who Won't Go On

Only a small fraction of souls have ever been ghosts, beyond the normal amount of time it takes for the new discarnate to adjust before leaving Earth. Our guides do not compel or coerce us to move into the spirit world if our unfinished business is so overpowering that we do not want to leave Earth's astral plane.

For most souls, the pulling sensation right after death is gentle and only grows more deliberate as we leave Earth's astral plane. There is no question that higher beings are instantly aware of our death. Yet the wishes of the deceased are respected. Keep in mind that time means nothing in the spirit world. Discarnates don't have a linear clock in their heads. So staying behind for days, months, or years doesn't have the same relevance as with incarnates. A ghost who has haunted an English castle for 400 years before finally returning to the spirit world may feel this amount of time as 40 days or even 40 hours.

Souls are not lost in some confined astral plane, and they do know that they have made a transition out of life on Earth. The ghost's confusion lies in the obsessive attachment they have to places, people, and events that they can't let go of. These actions of self-displacement are voluntary, but special guides called Redeemer Masters constantly watch for signs that the known disturbed spirits are ready to exit. From what Dr. Newton has observed, ghosts are less mature spirits who have trouble freeing themselves from earthly contaminations.

The most common cases of ghosts appear to involve souls who were murdered or wronged by another person in life.

There are also other entities who are not ghosts but won't go home after death. These entities simply don't want to be in contact with anyone. They live in a space they create for themselves. Some souls live in a nice place like a garden. Others – those who have harmed others, for instance – design terrible spaces for themselves like a prison, a room with no windows. In these spaces, they box themselves in so they can't make contact with anyone. It is a self-imposed punishment. But guides do give them time to sweat it out. This is a challenge for teachers. They know that these souls are concerned about their evaluations and the reactions from their soul groups. They are full of negative energy and are not thinking clearly. It may take many reassurances from those who wish to help them before these souls agree to give up their self-imposed places of confinement.

These people do not go to, nor experience, "purgatory." Purgatory, in Christian teaching, is not self-imposed. It is banishment, this experience is not the case. *Everything* is forgivable in the afterlife. All souls are repentant because they hold themselves accountable for their choices. Soul energy cannot be destroyed or made nonfunctional, but it can be reshaped and purified of earthly contamination. Souls who demand to be left in solitude after death on Earth are not self-destructing. Rather, some feel isolation is necessary out of concern for contaminating other souls with negative energy. There are also souls who don't feel contaminated, but they are not ready to be consoled by anybody.

After death, we have the right to refuse assistance from our spiritual masters for as long as we wish. This is a state of self-imposed space, a vacuum of subjective reality designed by the soul who wants to be alone. It's a separate space, away from the soul's spiritual center. These souls are not lost in some realm divided from the spirit world where others reside. The disjunction is mental.

Souls of silence know they are immortal, but they feel impotent. They consider what they do in solitude without help. They relive their acts over and over again, playing back all the karmic implications of what they have done to others and what has been done to them in their last life. They may have harmed others or have been harmed by them. Quite often, they feel victimized by events over which they had little control. They are sad and mad at the same time. They have no interaction with their soul groups. These souls suffer from self-recrimination and restricted insight. (These conditions fall within some of the definitions of purgatory.)

But in any case, these souls make up only a small fraction of the population of souls crossing over each day.

Discarnates Who Visit Earth

Some entities travel to Earth as tourists and have never incarnated on our planet. Some are quite advanced while others are maladapts. The character of these beings has been described as friendly, helpful, and peaceful. Likewise, they have also been described as distant, aggravating, and even contentious. Quite a number of Dr. Newton's subjects have told him that between their lives on Earth, they travel as discarnates to other worlds both in and out of our dimension.

Compared to Earth's population, only a tiny fraction of discarnates are here. There are times when only a few are around. It is not a constant thing; it's more cyclic.

There are no evil spirits, only inept ones ... and those who are careless ... and indifferent.

Possession

Dr. Newton's subjects do not see the devil or demonic spirits floating around Earth. What they do feel when they are spirits is an abundance of negative human energy exuding the intense emotions of anger, hate, and fear. These disruptive thought patterns are attracted to the consciousness of other negative thinkers who collect and disseminate even more disharmony. All this dark energy in the air works to the detriment of positive wisdom on Earth.

Dr. Newton has never once had a subject who was possessed by another spirit, unfriendly or otherwise. He says that he can come to no other conclusion than that *there is no such thing as possession of one spirit by another* when all of his subjects, even those who come to him with conscious beliefs in demonic forces, reject the existence of such beings when they see themselves as spirits.

The possibility that people can be possessed by a satanic being comes right out of medieval belief systems. It is fear-based and the result of theological superstition that has ruined countless lives over the last thousand years. Much of this nonsense has dissipated in the last 200 years, but it lingers with the fundamentalists. The exorcism of demons is still practiced by some religious groups. Frequently, clients who come to Dr. Newton with concerns about possession have lives that seem to be out of their control and filled instead with a variety of personal obsessions and compulsions. People who hear voices commanding them to do bad things are likely to be schizophrenic. They are not possessed.

Our physical world may have unhappy or mischievous spirits floating around, but they do not lock in and inhabit the minds of people. The spirit world is much too ordered to allow for such muddled soul activity. Beings possessed by other beings would not only abrogate our life contract but destroy free will. These factors form the foundation of reincarnation and cannot be compromised.

The idea that satanic entities exist as outside forces to confuse and subvert people is a myth perpetuated by those who seek to control the minds of others for their ends. Evil exists internally, initiated within the confines of the deranged human mind. Life can be cruel, but it is of our making here on this planet.

There are no soul monsters. **People are not born evil.** Rather, they are corrupted by the society in which they live, where practicing evil satisfies the cravings of depraved personalities. This emanates from the human brain. Studies on psychopaths have shown that the excitement of inflicting pain on others without remorse satisfies an emptiness they feel within themselves. Practicing evil is a source of power, strength, and control for inadequate people. Hate takes away the reality of a hateful life.

Evil is not genetic. Although, if a family has a history of violence and cruelty to their children, these acts are often passed on from one generation to the next as learned behavior. A soul's energy force may, during troubled times, dissociate from the body. Some feel they don't even belong to their bodies. There may also be influences of abnormal brain chemistry and hormonal imbalances affecting the central nervous system that might contaminate the soul. Immature souls often have difficulties handling the poor mental circuitry of disturbed human beings. However, souls don't represent all that is pure and good about a body, or they wouldn't be incarnating for personal development in the first place. Souls come to Earth to work on their own shortcomings.

Walk-ins

Dr. Newton writes that he believes the whole concept of walk-ins to be a false idea.

According to the proponents of this theory, tens of thousands of souls now on this planet come directly into their physical bodies without going through the normal process of birth and childhood. We are told that these possessing souls are enlightened beings who are permitted to take over the adult body of a soul who wants to check out early because life has become too difficult. Therefore, the walk-in soul is actually performing a humanitarian act, according to devotees of this theory. He calls this possession by permission.

Not one in all his years of working with thousands of subjects in regression has Dr. Newton ever had a walk-in soul. From all he has learned about body assignments, it takes years for a soul to fully meld its energy vibrations with that of a host brain. The process begins when the baby is in a fetal state after all. All the essential elements of who we really are come from the soul assigned to a specific body from the beginning. Consider first the three Is emanating from the soul: imagination, intuition, and insight. Then add such components as conscience and creativity.

Do you think the human mind is not going to recognize the loss of its partner Self to a new presence? That would drive a host body insane as opposed to healing it.

Souls take their responsibility very seriously, even to the extent of being inside nonfunctional bodies. They are not materially trapped.

For instance, a soul may inhabit a comatose host body for many years and not abandon it until death. These souls can roam freely across the land, visiting other souls who might be making brief trips away from their bodies during normal sleep states. This is especially true for souls in the bodies of babies. Souls are very respectful of their host body assignments even if they are bored. They leave a small portion of their energy so they can return quickly if needed. Their wavelengths are like homing beacons that have been "fingerprinted" on their human partners.

The Levels of Growth

There are five levels of spiritual growth exhibited here on Earth, and it is the very beginning of our long journey toward That Which Is. Dr. Newton tells us that he found *nearly three-quarters of humanity is still in the early stages of development.*

"For those who are curious, the percentages by soul level of all my cases are as follows: Level I, 42%; Level II, 31%; Level III, 17%; Level IV, 9%; and Level V, 1%. Projecting these figures into a world population of five billion souls would be unreliable, using my small sample. Nevertheless, I see the possibility we may have only a few hundred thousand people on Earth at Level V."

(Journey of Souls: Case Studies of Life Between Lives by Michael Newton © 2002 Llewellyn Worldwide, Ltd. 2143 Wooddale Drive, Woodbury, MN 55125.)

Rapid development is very rare on Earth. Many people have been back and forth here for 30,000 years now and are still in the lower parts of Level I and Level II.

After we have reached self-realization, we begin life tutored by older spirits until we have reached the ability to determine our future. The beginner soul may lead a number of lives here on Earth that are ineffective and confusing. It takes a lot of us a while to just get our bearings. If we don't produce, or if we make terrible mistakes, we go to a place for remolding ourselves when we return to heaven. By about the end of our fifth lifetime, we get the realization that we are part of a substantial group of spirits that are like us.

We won't know the level of our attainment in this world. In fact, it is wise to not even try. You will confuse yourself with things that don't matter, and it will be a waste of time. Spiritual development is not a drag; it is a delightful process. Nevertheless, it is extremely complex, and we can never get the full context of it in this life. Dr. Newton says that he had one subject who advanced very rapidly to Level III after only 4,000 years. This was an "outstanding performance."

The soul group to which we gravitate to is extremely important. It becomes the vehicle for our advancement. We gradually learn to ferret out those not especially like us, and to more and more – over lifetimes – join ourselves to our group.

This group jokes with us, and that humor leads to the exposure of hypocrisy and self-deception. Spiritual therapy groups offer us the support of others over time, of people who wish to advance, and of people who have learned to gently cajole us toward the understanding of our better selves. Our spiritual group is more like our family. Everyone has a personality, and not all are perfect. Everyone has a direction and a purpose: *advancement.*

But the individuals in these family groups have no hatred, no axe to grind, and no hidden agendas, suspicion, or distrust of others. There are no power struggles, just the determination to always do better. Souls don't distrust each other; they do sometimes distrust themselves and exhibit self-pride. It is the others who draw them out from their selves.

Some things happen in these groups that are hard to explain because they don't happen on Earth. One of those is the funnel of energy. When a group needs an adjustment or a renewal, those who watch over them provide a kind of sacred waterfall of energy, which washes over them, expands their thoughts, and returns them with added knowledge.

We are also connected to many subgroups with whom we work with. These groups work with us and with our group toward many mutually beneficial objectives. We may be lonely and disassociated on Earth, but we never are in heaven. We constantly experience the warmth of a loving family. We are just never bored with everyone having their own unique traits and contributing toward the enrichment of all.

Once we get past Level II, our soul group work is considerably reduced. In Levels III and IV, we may begin to serve as a guide ourselves, but only as a junior guide. But some find that they are unsuited to become guides. So, they go on to other work. This is interspersed between our lives here on Earth.

It should be noted that you have probably been thinking about yourself and wondering how you would fit in. You have probably been comparing yourself to others to see where you belong on the level of development. You may even have noticed a kind of jealousy toward those above you in development and a feeling of superiority over those below you. This kind of reaction is very human ... and *not at all* like our divine selves. There, we are never jealous of anyone else in our Life Between Lives. There is no animus whatsoever. We are just delighted to be where we are, and we find no disparagement or conflict with others over our station. The more advanced souls in this life have an advanced perception of the heavenly plan.

Perhaps this is because we are not in an organizational pyramid with supreme authority at the top. Rather, it is more like a long fabric with all the souls woven into it, like a moving continuum.

The more advanced we are, the happier we are. It would be a mistake to think that those who are more advanced and attain a kind of solitude are somewhat lonely. Advanced souls tell of having close friends, with whom they share intimate goals and achievements.

By the time we reach Level V, our talents are known. We either are a guide or we are not. But we have plenty of opportunities if the latter is the case. It is also the last tier on Earth, the last series of times we will be coming here. Level Vs have an expansive view of serving others. They are not interested in glory or the accumulation of physical things. They seem intent on helping others. That is not to say that they are perfect or have no faults. Otherwise, they would not be here. But their overall interest is in humanity, and they have a finely developed attunement toward assisting others. They have coping skills and exceptional insight coupled with an engaging serenity about them.

The hardest part to understand about our journey on Earth is that *addressing and overcoming pain is the path to advancement and growth.*

We on Earth do all we can to eliminate pain. We have 401(K)s, health insurance, and social security. We want a nest egg, annual vacations, etc. And yet – no matter what we do – we can never escape pain. It is SO frustrating! But if we knew what that pain could do for us, we would welcome it. Despite what we feel about life being long and burdensome, it is but a brief respite amid our eternal journey. It seems like forever, but it's just a micro-second.

I remember when I was a child and I stubbed my big toe on the sidewalk. I looked down and saw what I thought was a big chunk of meat hanging off. Amid all that blood, I thought, "Life as I knew it is over. I will never be the same. My body can no longer work perfectly." And yet, here I am – many decades later – and it is now but a faint memory.

So too is it for everything. Real life is long ... and beautiful. What we think is a life-changing experience is but a fleeting moment.

Our future becomes hazy beyond Level V. We are now going onward, but once we graduate from this world, we move on to another dimension. Very few Level VIs come to this planet. They do not need to. They are far too advanced to even have to.

Earth is considered a beautiful planet, but it is a place of physical discomforts and mental contests. What lies beyond is something we have little knowledge of. Some call it the World of All Knowing in which the senses of all living things are coordinated. Young souls do not go here. They are too immature. The further we develop, the more we are attracted to this World of All Knowing. But once we go there, we no longer come back here ... so we have no knowledge of it.

There are many other planets we go to for relaxation or just enjoyment. We have lives between Earth lives that are pure enjoyment. I don't know how we can fit so much in. We have only been active on this planet in force for perhaps 200,000 years. That is a lot of activity for a short period. It is not that we evolved into "humans," but that the introduction of the soul into the creatures on Earth brought about humanity. Souls made us totally human.

Souls work with the forces of creation. They gradually learn this too so that by the time they are firmly in Level III, they are expected to understand things like plant photosynthesis. In the beginning, they learn relationships between substances to develop the ability to unify energy. They form inanimate objects first. Later, they are encouraged to form miniature planetary systems for organisms that adapt to those environments. Not everyone has a knack for working with energy though. Those individual proclivities are like here on Earth. Everyone has a plethora of talents, and not everyone has the same talent or degree of interest for a talent.

By the time souls reach the intermediate levels, they begin to specialize in those major areas of interest where certain skills have been demonstrated.

Souls end their incarnations on Earth when they reach full maturity. Some have been incarnating for 30,000 years and are still only in the lower levels of Levels I and II.

Dr. Newton writes that he has no doubt that even higher levels of souls exist, but he has no knowledge of them because he only receives reports from people who are still incarnating. There are souls above Level VI, and they are highly venerated. They are superior beings, dark purple, and elusive. God is never seen.

> God is not He who is, but That which is.
> - Spinoza

We draw our existence from That which is, and so **we all share divine status**.

Dr. Newton says he could only go upstream so far because of the limitations of working with people still incarnating. Advanced subjects talk about the time of conjunction when they will join the "Most Sacred Ones." In this sphere of dense purple light, there is an all-knowing Presence. What all this means is something he cannot say, but he does know a Presence is felt when we go before our Council of Elders. Once or twice between lives, we visit this group of higher beings who are a step or two above our teacher-guides. This "Presence" is an energy force.

Dr. Newton says he is not fond of the term "level" to identify soul placement because this term clouds the diversity of development attained by souls at any particular stage. Despite these misgivings, it is his subjects who use the term "level" to describe where they are on the ladder of learning. They are also quite modest about these accomplishments.

In the spirit world, no soul is looked down upon as having less value than any other soul. We are all in a process of transformation to something greater than our current stage of enlightenment. Each of us is considered uniquely qualified to make some contribution toward the whole, no matter how hard we are struggling with our lessons. If this were not true, we would not have been created in the first place.

It would be easy to assume the ambiance of the spirit world is one of hierarchy. This conclusion would be quite wrong. If anything, the spirit world is hierarchical in mental awareness. We tend to think of organizational authority on Earth as represented by power struggles, turf wars, and the controlling use of a rigid set of rules within structure. There certainly is structure in the spirit world, but it exists within a sublime matrix of compassion, harmony, ethics, and morality far beyond what we practice on Earth. The spirit world also has a far-reaching centralized personnel department for soul assignments. Yet *there is a value system here of overwhelming kindness, tolerance, patience, and absolute love. Subjects are humbled by the process.*

Advancement through the taking of personal responsibility does not involve dominance of status ranking but rather is a recognition of potential. They see integrity and personal freedom everywhere in their Life Between Lives.

Most souls have an intense desire to prove themselves worthy of the trust placed in them. We are expected to make mistakes in this process. Souls have feelings of humility at having been allowed to incarnate in physical form.

Auras and Levels of Spiritual Attainment

Our aura IS us, and we could tell what level we are by our color if only we could see our true auras. Every soul has a specific color aura, beginning from when we are formed, which changes as we grow very slowly. Our auras are vibrational light patterns. Below are the levels of soul growth on Earth matched with their respective auras.

Levels: (description) / **% in each group** / **color characteristics**
    Level I (Beginner) 42% / White
    Level II (Lower Intermediate) 31% / white to light yellow
    Level III (Intermediate) 17% / solid yellow
    Level IV (Upper-Intermediate or Junior) 9% / yellow to light bule
    Level V (Advanced or Senior) 1% / light blue to light purple
    Level VI (Highly Advanced or Master) - / bluish purple w/ radiant light

The Three Most Commonly-Reported Character Traits for Each Color:

- Black: tainted, damaged, defiled negative soul energy, and in soul restoration centers
- White: purity, clarity, and restlessness
- Silver: ethereal, trust, and flexibility
- Red: passion, intensity, and sensitivity
- Orange: exuberant, impulsive, and openness
- Yellow: protective, strength, and courage
- Green: healing, nurturing, and compassion
- Brown: grounded, tolerant, and industrious
- Blue: knowledge, forgiveness, and revelation
- Purple: wisdom, truth, and divinity

    It takes many centuries for soul colors to change. The colors above are for the spirit world to see. We don't see them here. The human body changes the color of these energy patterns. When healers identify color auras around human beings, these colors are largely reflections of physical manifestations. Thus, colors in the spirit world are different than colors in the physical world.

The Four General Types of Souls

There must be many more types of souls, but these are the types that have been presented to Dr. Newton in his thousands of hypnotic reviews of Life Between Lives:

1. **Souls who are either unable or unwilling to function individually.** These souls usually work within collectives and never seem to leave the spirit world. Even so, all souls are allowed to experiment with existing in both the physical and mental universes.

2. **Souls who do not wish to incarnate in physical form.** They may not possess the requisite properties of light energy to engage in this activity. They seem to work only in mental worlds and appear to move easily between different dimensions. Most of their talents are beyond the comprehension of Dr. Newton's clients.

3. **Souls who incarnate only in physical worlds.** Some have the capability for training in mental spheres between lives but are not inclined to do so. They are not attracted to interdimensional travel, even during recreation. Quite a number of Dr. Newton's clients are in this category.

4. **Souls who have both the ability and desire to function in all types of physical and mental environments.** This does not necessarily give them more enlightenment than other soul types. Yet, their wide range of practical experience and

capabilities position them for many specialization opportunities involving varied assignments of responsibility.

These assemblages of more specialized souls are loosely knit at first as independent study groups. The training begins slowly and periodically with different specialized teachers. This allows an evaluation period for souls by their trainers. Souls who are testing the waters may leave these specialty groups while other promising candidates can be added. This practice is in opposition to the formation of long-term primary soul groups. The instruction becomes more intense as these new groups demonstrate that they can handle assignments. In these early stages, while souls are being weaned from their original groups, they still retain their regular guides and attend primary group functions. Independent study has a greater emphasis on self-direction by the soul in their tasks, which becomes even more pronounced as they develop into Level IV and V proficiency.

The Spirit World

Incarnation is an important tool. Some souls are driven more than others to expand and achieve their potential, but all of us will do so in the end. Being in many physical bodies and different settings expands the nature of our real self. This sort of *self-actualization of the soul* is the purpose of life in any world. Fulfillment is not cultivating the Self for selfish means but allowing for integration with others in life. That also shows character, integrity, and ethical conduct.

There is too much fear to overcome on Earth. There's too much conflict, too much diversity among too many people. Other worlds, meanwhile, have low populations with more harmony. Earth's population has outpaced its mental development. But for all that, we remain glad to come here because for all of Earth's quarreling and cruelty, there is passion and bravery here. It is, nevertheless, a difficult school.

Souls can be sent to any world with suitable life forms. Souls' planetary incarnations are not linked to Earth-like worlds or with intelligent bipeds who walk on land. They have a fondness for certain worlds and return to them, as some do to Earth, periodically for a succession of lives. Yet not many subjects can remember specific details about living in other worlds.

Once in a human body, *souls are not sent back down the mental evolutionary ladder.* Yet physical contrasts can be stark, and side trips away from Earth are not necessarily pleasant.

The ultimate objective of souls is to seek unification with the supreme source of creative energy. This Source *is* the spirit world. It is the ultimate selfless being that we strive to be.

When we were baby souls, we were thrust outward. As we are drawn back and as our adolescence faces challenges, we are drawn back inward. Our awareness begins at the edges of brilliant light. As we grow, we become more engulfed in the darker, purplish light. It is like watching the first flower of spring open, and the flower is you. As it opens more, you become aware of other flowers in a glorious field and there is unbounded joy.

The Spirit World Is Orderly and Structured

The spirit world simply cannot be compared to life on Earth. Souls are fully integrated by thought, but they may still suffer the consequences of their earthly actions. However, they are always protected, supported, and directed within the system by master souls (the spiritual management of souls).

Color, form, movement, and sound are individual markers of souls in their groups. These four elements appear to be interrelated. However, light energy, vibrational shapes and their wave movement, and the resonance of sound are not uniform among soul group members.

There is a language to sound in the spirit world that goes beyond the systemization of spoken language. Laughing, humming, chanting, and singing exist, as do the sounds of wind and rain, but they are indescribable. Some hypnosis subjects have difficulty producing spiritual names. These subjects say the names of souls in their minds consist of vibrational resonance which is impossible to translate. It gets even more complicated. One client stated, "In my experience, our real soul names are something similar to emotions, but they are not the emotions of humans, so I can't reproduce our names by any sound."

Everything on Earth and in the universe is apparently connected by thought waves to and from the spirit world. This may also be true for other dimensions near us as well. The multiple progression of intelligence with all elements of matter represents a symphony of order and direction based upon a plan of universal consciousness.

Memory

All past life memory is NOT genetic in origin or carried in our DNA cells from remote ancestors. The former bodies we had in prior lives are rarely genetically related to our current family. The average person has led past lives as Caucasians, Orientals, and Africans with no heredity connections. Moreover, how can our memories of being on other worlds in other species come from human DNA cells created only on Earth? The answer is simple. So-called genetic memory is soul memory emanating from the unconscious mind and *filtered in or through* the human brain in three categories:

1. **Conscious Memory.** This state of thought would apply to all memories retained by the brain in our biological body. It is manifested by a conscious ego Self that is perceptive and

adaptive to our physical planet. Conscious memory is influenced by sensory experiences and all our biological, primitive instinctual drives as well as emotional experiences. It can be faulty because there are defensive mechanisms related to what it receives and evaluates through impressions from the five senses.

1. **Immortal Memory.** Memories in this category appear to come through the subconscious mind. Subconscious thought is greatly influenced by body functions not subject to conscious control such as heart rate and glandular functions. However, it can also be the selective storeroom of conscious memory. Immortal memory carries the memories of our origins in this life and other physical lives. It is a repository of much of our psyche because the subconscious mind forms the bridge between the conscious and superconscious mind.

1. **Divine Memory.** These are the memories that emanate from our superconscious mind which houses the soul. If conscience, intuition, and imagination are expressed through the subconscious mind, they are drawn from this higher source. Our eternal soul-mind has evolved from superior conceptual thought energy beyond ourselves. Inspiration may seem to spring from immortal memory, but there is a higher intelligence outside our body-mind that forms a part of divine memory. The source of these divine thoughts is illusive. Sometimes, we conceive it as a personal memory. Actually, divine memory represents communication from beings in our immortal existence.

Other "Worlds"

The spirit world is the main center for learning, and it is the center for evaluation and analysis. But souls also rest there. There are other "worlds" (habitations for spiritual life) besides ours:

The "World" Without Ego (non-dimensional sphere)
It's the world of learning to be. It is for beginners, the place of our origin. Once given, the ego becomes a covenant between myself and the givers. The purpose of this world is the distribution of soul identity by advanced beings. The new soul starts out as congealed pure energy. The idea of "self" has not come into the new soul's consciousness. It is here that the soul is offered meaning to its existence. This creation of souls goes on continually. Because planets don't last forever, we are not necessarily slated for lives on Earth. Certain types of souls have an affinity for specific forms of physical life in the universe. Souls usually start out in an easy world or two then jump to this severe planet. Some worlds lean towards learning through physical contests while others prioritize mental contests. Earth has both. But the kinship humans have for each other, even as they struggle against each other through competing and collaborating at the same time, makes this an adventure for us and something we look forward to.

Humans are egocentric but vulnerable. They can make their character mean and yet have a great capacity for kindness. There is weak and courageous behavior on Earth. This diversity suits our soul. Those developing on Earth have a sanction to help humans know of the infinite beyond their lives and to assist them in expressing true benevolence through their passion. Having a passion to fight for life – that is what is so worthwhile about humanity. When humans experience trouble, they can be at their best and are quite noble.

Sometimes, if souls have developed severe obstacles to improvement, they return to the World Without Ego. But more about this was not drawn out of subjects very well by Dr. Newton.

The "World" of All Knowing (non-dimensional sphere)

This is the opposite of the World Without Ego, and not for young souls. It's a place of contemplation, the ultimate world of planning and design. It is the final destination of all thought. The senses of all living things are coordinated here. It is abstract in its highest form, blending content with form. It blends the rational with ideals, a dimension where the realization of all our hopes and dreams is possible. We get only bare references to this world of absolute because even advanced incarnated souls have no direct experience of it. All souls are anxious to reach here and be absorbed into it, especially as they draw closer and can see little bits of it. It can only be fully understood by souls above Level V.

The "World" of Altered Time (non-dimensional sphere)

This represents one's physical world. In the cases we study, it is Earth. The sphere of Earth is only simulated for those who use it. We don't physically live here, we only train here.

The "World" of Creation and Non-Creation

This is the only three-dimensional physical world.

It is not Earth. It's a little different. It's larger and somewhat colder with fewer oceans, but it's still similar. This world is in our universe but not in our Milky Way galaxy. We go to this other planet between Earth lives to create and to enjoy ourselves. There are no people there, and we roam among the forests, deserts, and oceans with no responsibilities alongside the small animals there. This is a vacation spot compared to Earth. There is no fighting, no bickering, or striving for supremacy. It is a pristine atmosphere, and all life is quiet. This "vacation" gives the soul an incentive to return to Earth and make it more peaceful too.

It is here that we learn to create by causing heat, pressure, and cooling from our energy flow and alternating currents of energy radiation. We transform things by playing with the frequency and dosages of energy. It's tricky and not too complicated. (If you thought nature did these things, who do you think nature is?) The souls here will have all incarnated on Earth previously. It is for our benefit that we help the creator in creating. We participate so that we can make contributions. We start creating in groups and use our energy with others and our instructor. Souls are expected to individually work with the forces of creation by the time they are solidly established in Level III. But it's not until they approach Level V do they begin to feel that they might contribute to the development of living things. Some souls have a natural gift for working with energy in creation. On the other hand, they may or may not be good guides.

A soul who becomes proficient with actually creating life must be able to split cells and give DNA instructions by sending particles of energy into the protoplasm and coordinating it with a sun's energy. Only the source, and perhaps the coordinated energy of the Old Ones, produces full-sized thermonuclear explosions which create physical universes and space itself. The supreme intelligence, called source, is made up of a combination of creators (the Old Ones) who fuse their energy to spawn universes.

The spirit world is not a pyramid. Rather, we are like threads in a long piece of fabric woven into it.

Other souls, who do not go to Earth, have other planets they visit for vacation where they can learn to create without any intelligent life around.

(Note: All animals have souls, but these souls are just simple fragments of mind energy. And we probably do not evolve from lesser animals.)

Timelessness

The spirit world is non-space and timeless, except in certain zones. These zones are interconnecting doors for us to pass through into a physical universe of time. These openings exist as thresholds between realities. The spirit world is a constant reality state as opposed to the shifting realities of dimensional worlds, which are material and changing. Past, present, and future only have meaning for souls living in the spirit world as a means of understanding succession in physical form. Living there is changelessness for those not crossing the thresholds into a universe of substance and time.

Chapter 8
What We Call "Hell" Is Not

Some souls act evil in this life, and they are separated from other souls for a time so that they can see what they chose and what would have been better for them to choose. Consistent errant souls who appear to be incorrigible, however, have their energy "rearranged." Other souls are reluctant to speak about this.

The returning energy of some souls, meanwhile, will not be sent back into their soul group right away. These are the souls who were contaminated by their physical bodies and became involved with evil acts. There is a difference between wrongdoing with no premeditated desire to hurt someone and intentional evil. The degrees of harm to others from mischief to malevolence are carefully evaluated.

Those souls who have been associated with evil are taken to special centers which some clients call "intensive care units." As Dr. Newton was told, their energy is remodeled to make it whole again. Depending upon the nature of their transgressions, these souls could be rather quickly returned to Earth. They might choose to serve as the victims of other's evil acts in the next life. Still, if their actions were prolonged and especially cruel over a number of lives, this would denote a pattern of wrongful behavior. Such souls could spend a long while in a solitary spiritual existence, possibly over a thousand Earth years. A guiding principle in the spirit world is that wrongdoing, intentional or unintentional, on the part of all souls will need to be redressed in some form in a future life. This is not considered punishment or even penance as much as an opportunity for karmic growth. There is no hell for souls, except perhaps on Earth.

Our thoughts, feelings, moods, and attitudes are mediated by body chemicals which are released through signals of perceived threats and danger. Fight or flight mechanisms come from our primitive brain, not from the soul. The soul has a great capacity to control our biological and emotional reactions to life, but many souls are unable to regulate a dysfunctional brain. Souls display these scars when they leave a body that has deteriorated in this fashion.

Dr. Newton has a theory for madness. The soul comes into the fetus and begins its fusion with the human mind by the time the baby is born. If this child matures into an adult with organic brain syndromes, psychosis, or major affective disorders, abnormal behavior is the result. The struggling soul does not fully assimilate. When this soul can no longer control the aberrant behavior of its body, the two personas begin to separate into a dissociated personality.

One of the red flags for souls who are losing their capacity to regulate deviant human beings is when they have had a series of lives in bodies demonstrating a lack of intimacy and displaying tendencies toward violence. This has a domino effect with a soul asking for the same sort of body to overcome the last one. Because we have free will, our guides are indulgent. A soul is not excused from responsibility for a disturbed human mind it is unable to regulate because it is a part of that mind. The problem for the slow learner soul is that they may have had a series of prior life struggles before occupying a body that escalated wrongdoing to a new level of evil. When these disturbed souls return to the spirit world, some subjects call the area to which they go to as the City of Shadows. It is here where the negative energy is erased.

Since this is the place where so many souls who have negative energy are gathered, it is dark to those outside of it. We can't go into this place with souls who have been associated with horror and who are undergoing alteration. We would not want to go there anyway. It is a place of healing. But from a distance, it has the appearance of a dark sea while I am looking at it from a bright, sandy beach. All the light around this area is brighter in contrast because positive energy defines the greater goodness of bright light.

When you get a chance to look into the darkness carefully, you will see that it is not black. It's a mixture of deep green. We know this is an aspect of the combined forces of the healers working here. We also know that souls who are taken to this area are not exonerated. Eventually, in some way, they must redress the wrongs they perpetrated on others. This they must do to restore full positive energy to themselves.

Not all of the more terrible memories of bad deeds are erased. It is known that if the soul did not retain some memory of an evil life, it would not be accountable. This knowledge by the soul is relevant for future decisions. Nevertheless, the resurrection of the soul in the spirit world is merciful. The soul mind does not fully retain all the lurid details of harming others in former host bodies after treatment. If this were not true, the guilt and association with such lives would be so overpowering to the soul that they might refuse to reincarnate again to redress these wrongs. These souls would lack the confidence to ever dig themselves out of pits of despair.

But there are souls whose acts in host bodies were so heinous that they are not permitted to return to Earth.

Some lives are so difficult that the soul arrives home tired. Despite the energy rejuvenation process initiated by our guides who combine their energy with ours at the gateway, we may still have a depleted energy flow. In these cases, more rest and solitude may be called for rather than celebrations. Indeed, many souls who desire rest receive it before reunification with their groups. Our soul groups may be boisterous or subdued, but they are respectful of what we have gone through during an incarnation. All groups welcome back their friends in their own way with deep love and camaraderie.

As much as we would like to avoid it – and we *would* like to avoid it – no discussion of heaven is complete without a discussion of hell. So much of contemporary spirituality concentrates on the beauty that is always within, on the reality that God never lets us go no matter what we do, and that our inevitable desire and conclusion is to be one with God forever. Because of this, when we first get into this study, we may tend to bypass hell and treat it as nonexistent. Also, the old-time concept of hell was a place of eternal punishment. And we know now that hell cannot be eternal punishment since we are always individuated manifestations of God's Self. And we can always change.

But this place where we live our earthly life is designed for choice and for experiences, and experiences always have embedded consequences. We are a compilation of our choices, which lead to experiences, which lead to memories. We cannot avoid the poor choices we make as if they made no difference. There is a wide gap between choosing to be our best selves and choosing to be our lesser or more selfish selves.

In this life, our decisions set our vibrational level. When we pass to the other side of this life, we will have already established a vibrational pattern over time. That vibrational pattern resonates with states of existence on the other side, as in one skein. We are not rewarded or punished for our deeds. Rather, we gravitate to the vibrational pattern we had established in life. There is no condemnation or punishment for our lesser decisions, but we simply consign ourselves to the place of the comfort level we have chosen. That place, should we have made poor choices of selfishness or hurt others, will bring us to a level that is painful in that it is distant from our rightful reality of being perfect manifestations of God. We simply stay in that place – "hell," if you like – until we decide that it does not represent our best selves, that it's not the best expression of who we want to be, and that it's not a satisfactory presentation of our true selves.

That is what is meant by those who say, "heaven is here." In "heaven" we will live in the vibrational milieu we establish here on Earth.

Some call this place hell because we have always had a Hell in our imagined history, and this is the closest we get to that. But it is not condemnation, not punishment, not Evil-Getting-Even. It doesn't even hurt. It is a place where we go through a rather extensive re-orientation, a re-adjustment of just about everything. We stay there for a while too until we have been re-aligned.

It should be noted – surprisingly – that we do not eschew going to this hell. We know that it is the best place to get back to our true selves after a life of forgotten misuse of our innate talents.

"Hell" is not eternal, because we always have the option to change our minds and move on. It can be, however, a state of profound pain and emptiness void of love and compassion, which is the very stuff that defines us as expressions of Loving Consciousness. How long we stay there is completely up to us. Lifetimes that put a person into deeper and deeper hell repeatedly become more and more difficult to erase and change.

Souls who have made choices not to be their higher selves, depending on the severity, persistence, and ramifications of those choices, will find themselves in this hell to examine what it is that they did that caused them such pain. They are there to saturate themselves with the results of giving expression to their lesser selves. What were those misjudgments, miscalculations, abuses, and selfish actions – which we call "sin" – that brought us this pain? Do we want to keep this up? (We can, if we so choose.) When we decide we should change because such actions always bring us suffering in the long run, we then get the chance to enter another lifetime and be given those same kinds of choices. But we do not get out of hell until we have decided that we do indeed want to change for the better.

Can some among us continue to make such poor choices through multiple lifetimes over and over again that we lose our differentiated souls? Can a soul, which once upon a time stood as Light/Energy concentrated enough to be individuated and seek the experience of earthly creativity to enhance its theoretical knowledge of its perfection, make such profoundly selfish choices that it loses its differentiation within the Wholeness that is God/Loving Consciousness before no longer existing as an individuated manifestation of God (e.g., though the energy would remain within the One, the differentiation would not)? I have to say that I am not sure, but I fear that it is so. Our choices for our higher selves or our lesser selves are profoundly important.

Just as hell is the attraction of negative vibrational patterns, so too is heaven the attraction of positive vibrational patterns. Each is a place where the positive (heaven) or negative (hell) life that we have led is seeped into our deepest being and the lessons of it have been learned. In hell, we yearn to return to Earth to be given another chance to do it right this new time. In heaven, we remain until the joys, goodness, and compassion we may have chosen in the past lifetime have sunk in and their lessons have been learned. If we have advanced far enough, we leave heaven to either return to Earth for another life or we progress upward to ever-closer oneness with the All-Loving Awareness. If we have not finished our earthly learning experiences, we take the opportunity to select a new set of circumstances on Earth to which to reincarnate.

Hell is just as real as heaven, and it is not a place anybody would ever want to go to. Plenty still do, at least temporarily.

On the other hand, we learned in the section above on hybrid souls that they can gravitate, by their choices, to become atrocity souls. This may cause their own soul energy to be disseminated. This would end their individuality and end their individual existence. So, in that case, and probably in other cases where the soul has chosen so much evil and inflicted it on others, they may be un-salvageable. There are those rare occasions when a soul's energy is disseminated, where only a small particle of the original soul's energy is mixed with new energy and given a new start. With this fresh beginning, the new soul could begin leading a productive life on Earth and elsewhere.

So, to that limited extent, when all else has been tried and failed, there is a hell.

Chapter 9
Questions and Observations

Do Animals Have Souls?

Animals have individual personalities, feelings, and even a sense of the needs of their owners. Animals provide comfort during our bereavement and physical illnesses. Pets can lift our spirits and foster healing while providing us with love and companionship without reservations. If animals have thought perceptions, then they have individualized energy at some level. Every animal has its particular classification of intelligent energy.

Dr. Newton's clients have told him that all animals do indeed have soul energy. They are not like human souls, however, and also differ from one another. After death, the energy from these animals reportedly exists in different spheres from that of the human soul. The souls of all living things have different properties. Animal souls have smaller particles of energy. They have less volume and are not as complex and multifaceted as the human soul. Animal souls are not ego-driven. They are not as overwhelmed by identity issues as we are. They also accept and blend with their environment rather than fighting to control it like human beings. We can learn from them. Domesticated animals can extend love and affection to humans, which we need. Wild animal souls are not as focused in this area.

When a soul in the spirit world wants the pleasure of an animal he had on Earth, he has to call for that animal as animals don't normally live in the same spaces as human souls. A human soul cannot go to the animal's place. An Animal Caretaker, called a "tracker," must bring them to the soul. Various animals have community bonding by general species (whales, dolphins, and seals ... crows and hawks ... horses and zebras, etc.), which the soul in the spirit world generally does not understand. An Animal Caretaker has the skill to track and find the spark of soul energy that would not have died from our animal on Earth. They would then reconstruct that animal exactly as the soul knew him on Earth. The pet will know the soul and be able to play with him whenever he wishes, and then he will go.

Suicide

Human extravagance has no bounds when it comes to instilling fear like the terrible punishment said to be coming for those who commit suicide. This has been a deterrent, but it is certainly the wrong approach. The first thing physically fit people who commit suicide usually say after death is, "How could I have been so *stupid*!" Suicide by a person, young or old, whose physical state has reduced the quality of their life to almost nothing is treated differently in the spirit world than those who had healthy bodies. While all suicide cases are treated with kindness and understanding, people who kill themselves with a healthy body do have a reckoning. When there is unendurable physical suffering, we have the right to be released from the pain and indignity of being treated like helpless children connected to life-support systems. In the spirit world, no stigma is attached to a soul leaving a terribly broken body and who is released by its own hand or from that of a compassionate caregiver.

People who say they don't belong here on Earth need to be taken seriously. They may be potential suicide cases. These clients fall into one of three spiritual classifications:

1. Young, highly sensitive souls who began their incarnations on Earth but have spent little time here. Certain souls in this category have had great difficulty adjusting to the human body. They feel their very existence to be threatened because it is so cruel.

1. Both young and older souls who incarnated on another planet before coming to Earth. If these souls lived on worlds less harsh than Earth, they may be overcome by the primitive emotions and high density of the human body. Essentially, they feel they are in an alien body.

1. Souls below Level III who have been incarnating on Earth since their creation but are in host bodies whose physical ego mind is radically different from their immortal soul. They cannot seem to find themselves in this particular lifetime.

When those with healthy bodies commit suicide, they feel somewhat diminished in the eyes of their guides and group peers because they broke their covenant in a former life. There is a loss of pride from a wasted opportunity. Life is a gift, and a great deal of thought has gone into allocating certain bodies for our use. We are the custodians of this body and that carries a sacred trust. It is a contract. When a young, healthy person commits suicide, our teachers consider this an act of gross immaturity and the abrogation of responsibility. Our spiritual masters have placed their trust in our courage to finish life with functional bodies in a normal fashion, no matter how difficult. They have infinite patience with us, but with repeated suicide offenders, their forgiveness takes on another tone.

In suicide cases involving healthy bodies, one of two things generally happens to these souls. If they are not a repeat offender, the soul is frequently sent back to a new life rather quickly, usually at their request, to make up for lost time. This could be within five years of their death on Earth. The average soul is convinced that it is important to get right back on the diving board after having taken a belly flop in a prior life.

For those who display a pattern of bailing out when things get rough, there are places of repentance for a good purpose. These are not horrible places. These souls volunteer to go to a beautiful planetary world with water, trees, and mountains, but with no other life. They have no contact with other souls in these places of seclusion except for sporadic visits by a guide to assist them in their reflections and self-evaluation. Places of isolation come in many varieties which we here may consider to be terribly boring. But perhaps that is the idea.

While you are sitting out the next few games on the bench, your teammates are continuing with the challenges in their new lives. Apparently, this medicine seems to work because these souls come back to their groups feeling refreshed. At the same time, they also come back recognizing that they have missed a lot. Nonetheless, there are souls who will never adjust to Earth. Some are reassigned to other worlds for their future incarnations.

While it is true that we are given our bodies by an act of divine creation, everyone's life belongs ultimately to them. The right to die is a hotly debated topic in legal circles today, especially as it pertains to doctor-assisted suicide with the terminally ill. It has been said that if death is the final act of life's drama, and we want that last act to reflect our own convictions during life, we should have the right regardless of the religious or moral convictions of a majority. The opposing view is that if life is a gift, of which we are the custodians, we have certain moral duties despite our own feelings. Dr. Newton suggests that knowing what he does about how our souls choose life, with the free will to make changes during that life, he believes we have the right to choose death when no quality of life remains and there is no possibility of recovery. It is not intended that the degradation of our humanity be prolonged.

Abortion

Dr. Newton never had a single case where a soul joined the fetus in the first trimester because there was not enough brain tissue for them to work with. One client told him that he never entered the baby until after the sixth month. Another client told him he never enters the baby until the eighth month when the brain is larger and when he has more to work with during the coupling.

When souls first enter the human brain, they talk (telepathically) with the baby. The soul comes to give the child depth of personality.

Its being is enhanced by the soul's presence. Without the soul, the human brain would largely function as unripened fruit. The human brain recognizes this and is glad to see the soul.

The soul talks to the human body as a second entity up to the age of six. It is better not to force a full meld right away. They play games as two people for a while.

There is a universal consciousness of life surrounding all unborn babies. The creative force of existence is never separated from any form of living energy. A fetus can be alive as an individual entity without yet having an immortal soul identity. If a mother aborts her child in the first trimester, there are loving spiritual forces hovering nearby to comfort this mother and watch over the child. Even in cases of miscarriages and abortions between four and nine months, souls can be in place to support both the child and mother in a more direct physical manner with energy. Souls know in advance the probability of the baby going to term.

When a mother loses her child for whatever reason, the odds are quite high that the soul of this baby will return again to the same mother with her next child. If this mother does not bear another child, the soul may return to another close member of the family because that was the original intent. When life is short, souls call these filler lives, and they too have a purpose for the parent.

The soul will receive the mother's emotional feelings during pregnancy more than her clear thoughts. That's how the soul knows if the baby is wanted or not, and this makes a difference in the baby getting a good or bad start.

The debate about abortion on Earth is between those religious persons who say all life is sacred and no one has the option of taking what God has given and those who say that it is the mother's decision because it is her body. But it is more complicated than most people realize because of this layer of understanding that every soul is immortal and has a purpose even if it's quite a short period and not understood by others. Many others among us, thinking they are devout Christians, believe that we should never thwart God's will. But *we can never "thwart God's will."* It requires, if we can understand, that we apply these new layers of thought and understanding gleaned from our awareness of the eternality of life. It requires understanding of how our free choices, no matter what they are so long as they are made with openness to the universe as we understand it, are valid and beneficial to our growth process.

Every individual does indeed have the final say over themselves and their bodies. But the process and purpose of life on Earth require that we should look at all the circumstances surrounding the possible abortion.

Gays and Lesbians and Other Sexual Types

At Levels I and II, many souls choose bodies of one particular gender around 75 percent of the time because they are comfortable being male or female. **Gay and lesbian** clients have started the process of alternating gender choices in their lives, which is reflective of the more developed soul. Choosing to be a gay male or lesbian female is one means of affecting that transition in a particular life. Thus, their current sex may not be as familiar to them as the body of the opposite sex, such as a gay man feeling as if he is actually in the body of a female.

The second and far more important factor is souls choosing a gay or lesbian orientation in advance of the life they are now living because they deliberately chose to exist in a society that would be prejudiced against them. Dr. Newton's gay and lesbian clients are usually not young, inexperienced souls. If they go public, this means these people have decided to live a life where they will be swimming upstream in a culture with rigid gender role stereotypes but these perceptions and prejudices are now changing substantially. They must try and rise above public abuse to find self-esteem and self-identity. This takes daring and resolve.

The Future on Earth

The question has been fairly asked about why spiritual life has been loosened to permit such research into the spirit world. Dr. Newton says he thought about this a lot: why now? He believes now, in the 21st century, younger hypnotherapists will go far beyond what his generation has been able to accomplish in unlocking the spiritual mind. The reasons for our ability to discover more of the mysteries about life on the other side is a direct outgrowth of living in the 20th century.

> "The day science begins to study non-physical phenomena, it will make more progress in one decade that in all the previous centuries of its existence.
> - Nikola Tesla (1856-1943)

Never before have such a variety of drugs been so pervasive in the human population. These mind-altering chemicals imprison the soul within a body encumbered by a mental fog. The soul's essence is unable to express itself through a chemically addicted mind. The planners on the other side have lost patience with this aspect of human society. There are other reasons as well, as Dr. Newton saw it. We live in a frantic, rage-filled, overpopulated, and environmentally degraded world. The mass destruction of our planet in the last hundred years from all sources is unequaled in human experience.

Dr. Newton does not have a dark vision of the future despite these conclusions. The world is a far better place than decades ago in many ways. However, *we are witnessing the eroding of individualism and human dignity in an overcrowded society dominated by materialism.* Globalization, urban sprawl, and bigness are a formula for loneliness and disassociation. Many people believe in nothing but survival. In some ways, humanity is fighting back.

There are too many people trying to escape from reality because they do not see their identity as having purpose or meaning. **Drugs and alcohol aside, in overcrowded and high-tech societies around the world, people have an emptiness of spirit because they are ruled by their body-ego senses. They have little or no connection to their real Self.**

By Dr. Newton's thinking, that would be the reason for humanity getting this injection of purpose in seeing Life Between Lives: to offset the current escape from reality.

Other Universes

There are other universes besides the one which contains Earth. We can, and do, enter various rooms of different physical realities from spiritual doorways.

(Here I again deviate from Dr. Newton:) Science tells us that there are 11 dimensions. But we now live in a world of only four dimensions (up/down, right/left, forward/backward, and time). Science tells us that these unknowns (to us) are "tucked under" in this universe. We have absolutely no experience, no understanding ... no idea ... of what other universes with other dimensions might be. Might there be a "universe" of music? Might there be a "universe" of mathematics?

Dr. Newton says that he has the feeling that universes other than our own are created to provide environments suitable for the growth of souls with beings we can't even imagine. One subject told Dr. Newton about a "paradise planet" with fewer people and a quieter, simpler version of Earth. This planet was not far from Earth and it was not in our universe, but it's closer to Earth than many planets in our galaxy. Souls are not limited by the dimensional constraints of our universe.

Chapter 10
The Source

The source, which is perfect already, chooses to create further intelligence which is less than perfect to help it create. In this way, by self-transformation and rising to higher plateaus of fulfillment, we add to the building blocks of life. The source creates for fulfillment of itself. The source is all that we can know, and we think what this creator desires is to express itself through us by birthing. The creator's perfection is maintained and enriched by sharing the possibility of perfection with us, and this is the ultimate extension of itself. Perhaps if the source did not create souls to nurture and grow, its sublime energy would shrink from a lack of expression.

This source – hinted at but never seen or interacted with at the level of perfection (or rather the lack of perfection) all souls still incarnating on Earth have attained – is everything. There is nothing in existence or potentially in existence which is not it.

In his three books under the opening banner *Conversations with God*, Neale Donald Walsh confounded his readers with the announcement that "God" said there are many Gods beyond God. This was so confounding, in fact, that it was passed over by many because it made no sense to the foundation humanity had built for itself in its recent recorded history.

Hypnotic regressions take individuals back to their home base, their spiritual life, in which each physical lifetime can be compared to a mere drop in an eternal ocean. It is all present within us by the process by which our soul is formed out of the wholeness of unbridled energy that we call Divinity (that sort of congeals itself out of the spiritual energy that is "God" into an individuated concentration that achieves self-recognition). It then goes on over thousands of years to gain self-understanding and perfection through trials, temptations, challenges, and difficulties – all to be overcome in the process of strengthening those virtues within that are indeed themselves Divine. We find that we have many hundreds or thousands of lifetimes. We can move from a new and inexperienced soul into a practiced and experienced soul who achieves as much perfection as this physical set of experiences can provide.

And then we move on to other forms of expression, other journeys toward greater perfection, and higher realms of light, joy, and beauty.

Those higher realms can only be glanced at through the prism of our current soul development. We are not there yet, and we cannot see beyond the realm in which we now mature. But we are told by our guides, by higher teachers, and by others who take a step into them and return for a visit that they are there. They are the next steps to which we ultimately aspire.

This is not a quick journey. But it is a rich, magnificent, enthralling, and electrifying process of perfection that continually enlivens us with new understanding, new goals, new beauty and joy, and the taste of yet ever more to come. We may not be able to see this long-distance path from the perspective of this life, but we truly do love it. We yearn for it.

And ... we'll never be bored!

Each of the levels, to which we now aspire and to which we see vaguely beyond and towards, seems from a lower perspective to be what we call "God." But we now know enough to know that the Sum Total of Perfection, which radiates waves of its partial force of existence outwards/inwards to growing expressions, is beyond our vision and our comprehension. It's beyond the expression we are presently capable of understanding. We are on our way toward it, though. We are on our way toward BEING ONE WITH IT, in fact. But we are not there now, and we cannot see more than its beautiful magnetic force. Its drawing power is sublime and divine! We will actually never arrive there, because that Power is itself forever growing by absorbing the growth of all its components. But *we will love this eternal process.*

"Lord, you have made us for yourself,
and our hearts are restless

until they rest in You."
- St. Augustine of Hippo, Fourth Century

Traditional Christian Teaching
"God" is taught to be Trinity.

The Trinity, as generally conceived today (if at all) would be more like the source which is the "Ultimate From-Which." The FATHER, "THE FIRST PERSON OF THE TRINITY," is the Begetter, the Instigator, the Creator of all that is from within its unbounded fecundity. THE SON, "THE SECOND PERSON OF THE TRINITY," is the Outflow of that source (what is evident, seen, and unseen) and the product resulting from that unbounded fecundity. And the HOLY SPIRIT, "THE THIRD PERSON OF THE TRINITY," is the movement of that source which manifests itself as all the Outflow.

Journey of Souls and *Destiny of Souls* have a deep DIVINE impact. Dr. Newton's work is a more full-throated involvement of Divinity in the physical world than "traditional" Christianity, or often many other religious systems, ever had. Using an analogy, there is a difference between traditional religious conceptualizations about the divine-human relationship.

The traditional conception is the "pulling of strings," where God is like a "Santa Clause" or a divine vending machine where human beings ask for favors. For example, "Oh, God, please let my mother live through this cancer." or "If you would only do this for me now, I promise to do, etc." Dr. Newton's phenomenological account of subjects in a state of hypnosis, however, attributes the divine-human relationship as a COMPLETE immersion in Divine purpose.

In Dr. Newton's works, the soul, which might be characterized as an "individuated being" while in the Earthy plane, is always safe and never threatened. The soul has a relationship with the Divine (in that Divinity is its constant source), one that is always loving although still "challenged" by "opportunities" to grow, develop, and adapt in the direction of the Divine. Although the soul might be seen as beset with problems, there are still pathways for growth and opportunities to make decisions and choices. The divine-human relationship is always a union. I do not perceive this to be true in traditional Christian perspectives.

We Want to Become God

I don't think there can be any certitude until we "become" God ... which is really what we all want to do and be: to become the perfection of who we are. We want to reach our potential. And our potential and direction is always the source. But just as we are individually growing in knowledge and experiences, so is this Loving Consciousness *which incorporates all of every one of its individuated manifestations' (souls) growing and learning* experiences and memories. The universal consciousness itself is changing and growing. So, while we aspire toward it and constantly grow toward being it, we can never achieve it because it is growing at a much faster and broader pace.

Thank God (no pun intended). What would ever happen if this were not the case and we could eventually catch up and become the Source? Would we evaporate and lose our individuality as our consciousness would be absorbed into that of the Source? I don't want to think about the consequences of that, and I don't have to because it cannot happen.

Buddhism appears to be similar to true Christianity, at least in the way that it seems to be a primitive and early understanding of our human condition and destined to be built upon. It must be quite sad for a Buddhist to determine that he or she has NO ultimate future, is destined for oblivion (and sometimes through torturous existences), and would just disappear. What was it all worth?

I think Buddhists must see the Source as never changing, never growing, and never expanding. When the individual follower of Buddha achieves his/her nirvana, he/she just disappears. Not a happy ending!

All that we see is, in a way, an illusion. We are here ONLY for the experiences ... we create nothing that lasts outside of our memories and souls. Of course, as we create buildings, products, systems, and all other types of "creations" in this world, we create "etheric" creations at the same time as well. For example, when I think of how to make a table – perhaps because I have done it before – I think first of all of its etheric form (that form in my consciousness which is the blueprint). That exists before the physical or actual table ever does, and after that table might be destroyed. Etheric creations continue throughout our existence. For as long as we exist, we will have that etheric blueprint.

This has importance for each individual way beyond their "successes" in this life. Let me use myself as an example. As I mentioned at the beginning of this book, I believe I am a very creative individual, always looking forward and not backward. I'm able to see what things around me should be in the future. This does not mean I am successful in conveying this to others, or even successful in this life's terms. I have probably had 100 ideas (or maybe 500) that have NOT come to fruition – usually after long planning on how to make them a successful endeavor – for every one of them that has made it "successfully" and complete.

That doesn't matter. What matters is that I have created them in my mind. They will forever be in my eternal soul in "blueprint" form. As I progressed, whether or not they became fulfilled, I became more proficient in fleshing them out and detailing the steps to make them a "success." Sure, it might have been nice if I had the money to bring them to fruition or to convince others to invest in them. But, in fact, I rarely did. Most never made it to the light of day. Maybe they should *not* have. Maybe I might have gotten arrogant or more selfish if they had. I will never know (except perhaps in my life reviews or studies of them in Life Between Lives on the other side). What I do know is that those pursuits have enriched my life here. I don't know why but thank God I had all those this-world-unfulfilled opportunities.

Moreover, even if I had been successful (in this life's terms) in 500 of those "brilliant" ideas, I would be able to take exactly zero of them with me into the life beyond. Anything physical remains in this physical world, only to be reconverted to energy again within a few hundred years. The ONLY things that do remain are those blueprints in my mind.

There is ONLY Loving Consciousness, this Loving Consciousness which *moves*. We don't have a full understanding of consciousness, but we do know that if it were sedentary, it would not exist. The *movement of* consciousness is called "energy" from one perspective (science), and "spirit" from another (religious thought). But it is exactly the same thing. It is the only reality, and everything is individuated manifestations WITHIN it. There is ONLY **ONE**, only God, only Loving Consciousness, and only All-Loving Awareness. Everything that is exists within it as a manifestation of it.

Further, there can be no certitude until we "become" God. That is really what we all want to do and be in becoming the perfection of who we are and reaching our potential. Simultaneously, just as we individually are growing in knowledge and experiences, so is this Loving Consciousness *which incorporates all* of every one of its individuated manifestations, souls, growing and learning experiences, as well as memories. This consciousness is changing and growing.

We come into this world having chosen our predispositions and having our growth issues to work on, so our interpretation of events will differ from life to life. Certain aspects of them are beyond our control WHILE HERE, but they are very much WITHIN our control on the Other Side BEFORE we get here. We set things up to choose the best (even if we often do not do that, and we then have to come back and try again next time).

These are **not** the only two choices: 1) Zeus, or any other god pulling the strings, or 2) chance. Loving Consciousness is so much more intimately involved in every aspect of this world. And yet, it leaves it to us to make our choices and learn because WE set up every experience in our life. Many people wail "It's not fair!" or feel they are victims ... and this is simply not so. Every individual chooses every challenge he/she will have in their future life. We sometimes take on a great deal, but we know in advance that we can take it. The greater the set of problems, the greater the chance of faster advancement. That's the way God set this world up!

Chapter 11

The Impact of Dr. Newton's New Perspective

A major aspect of our mission on Earth as souls is to mentally survive being cut off from our real home.

All the accounts of life after death in Dr. Newton's case files, he says, have no traditionally scientific foundation to prove the statements of these subjects. His cases report that our souls are born of a creator who places a peaceful state deliberately out of reach so we will strive harder.

We learn from wrongdoing. The absence of good traits exposes the ultimate flaws in our nature. That which is not good is testing us. Otherwise, we would have no motivation to better the world through ourselves, and no way to measure advancement.

For this magnificent reason, we can see that the foundational basis of most world religions – guilt and sin – is false. **Dr. Newton's subjects tell us that the purpose of our journeys on this planet and others is to experience what we call "sin" as not pleasing to us over the long run. Once realized, we change to no longer wanting such experiences of "sin." Once that realization has occurred, those "sins" become absolute blessings for us.** *That is the purpose of our existence as human beings and the purpose of the entire universe and, most probably, many others.*

The foundational aspects of religions teach that God is offended by such sins, that when we do sin we gravely offend God, and He is therefore justified in punishing us for such sins. That is outright wrong. We come here to be tested, to experience for ourselves that what we naively thought to be rewards to us for bad behavior were not that. They were things that took us in the wrong direction. We only felt better when we stopped doing such things. What a great reality!

In a remarkable underlying message, particularly from advanced subjects, the possibility is held out that the God-oversoul of our universe is on a less-than-perfect level. Thus, complete infallibility is deferred to an even higher divine source.

Earth is one of countless worlds with intelligent beings, each with its own set of imperfections to bring into harmony. Extending this thought further, we might exist as one single-dimensional universe out of many, each having its own creator governing at a different level of proficiency in levels similar to the progression of souls seen in Dr. Newton's works.

If the souls who go to planets in our universe are the offspring of a parent oversoul who is made wiser by our struggle, then could we have a more divine grandparent who is the absolute God? The concept that our immediate God is still evolving, as we are, takes nothing away from an ultimate source of perfection who spawned our God. To Dr. Newton's mind, a supreme, perfect God would not lose omnipotence of total control over all creation by allowing for the maturation of less-than-perfect Gods as a final means of edification so that we might join with the ultimate God.

Pain in life is especially insidious because it can block the healing power of our souls, especially if we have not accepted what is happening to us as a preordained trial. Yet, throughout life, our karma is designed so that each trial will not be too great for us to endure.

We are divine but imperfect beings who exist in two worlds, material and spiritual. It is our destiny to shuttle back and forth between these universes through space and time while we learn to master ourselves and acquire knowledge. We must trust in this process with patience and determination. Our essence is not fully knowable in most physical hosts, but the Self is never lost because we always remain connected to other worlds.

Honesty, humor, and love are the primary foundations of our life after life.

Large numbers of souls who have had more frequent incarnations in recent centuries on Earth are opting, when they get the chance, for less stressful worlds. There are enlightened places where amnesia is greatly reduced without causing homesickness for the spirit world. As we approach the next millennium, the masters who direct Earth's destiny appear to be making changes to permit more information and understanding of who we are and why we are here to come into our lives.

The most significant benefit that comes from knowing we have a home of everlasting love waiting for us is being receptive to the higher spiritual power within our minds. The awareness that we do belong somewhere is reassuring and offers us peace, not merely as a haven from conflict, but to unify ourselves with a universal mind. One day, we are going to finish this long journey – all of us – and reach an ultimate state of enlightenment where everything is possible.

~

As Doctor Newton says:

"Because each of us is a unique being, different from all others, it is incumbent upon those who desire internal peace to find their own spirituality. When we totally align ourselves to belief systems based upon the experience of other people ... we lose something of our individuality in the process. The road to self-discovery and shaping a personal philosophy not designed by the doctrines of organizations takes effort but the rewards are great.

"If there is no inner peace, it does not matter what sort of spiritual affiliation you have. Disengagement in life arises when we separate ourselves from our inner power by taking the position that we are all alone, without spiritual guidance, because no one upstairs is listening ... On the road of life, we must take responsibility for all our decisions without blaming other people for life's setbacks that bring unhappiness.

"You were not given your body by a chance of nature. It was selected for you by spiritual advisors and after previewing their offerings of other host bodies, you agreed to accept the body you now have. Thus, <u>you are not a victim of circumstance</u>. You are entrusted with your body to be an active participant in life, not a bystander. We must not lose sight of the idea that we accepted this sacred contract of life and this means the roles we

play on Earth are actually greater than ourselves ... the only limitations to personal insight are self-imposed.

"Everyone on this planet has a personal spiritual guide. Spirit guides speak to our inner mind if we are receptive. While some guides are more easily reached than others, each of us can call upon and be heard by these guides.

"That which is meaningful in life comes in small pieces or large chunks all at one time. Self-awareness can take us beyond what we thought was our original destination. Karma is the setting in motion of those conditions on our path that foster learning. The concept of a Source orchestrating all of this need not be pretentious. The spiritual externalist waits for reunification with a Creator after death, while the internalist feels part of a Oneness each day. Spiritual insight comes to us in quiet, introspective, subtle moments which are manifested by the power of a single thought.

"It is vital to our mental health that we laugh at ourselves and the foolish predicaments we get into along the road. Life is full of conflicts and the struggle, pain and happiness we experience are all reasons for our being here. Each day is a new beginning."

One of Dr. Newton's subjects concluded: "Coming to Earth is about traveling away from our home to a foreign land. Some things seem familiar, but most are strange until we get used to them, especially in conditions which are unforgiving. <u>Our real home is a place of absolute peace, total acceptance, and complete love.</u> As souls separated from our homes, we can no longer assume these beautiful features will be present around us. On Earth, we must learn to cope with intolerance, anger, and sadness while searching for joy and love. We must not lose our integrity along the way, sacrificing goodness for survival and acquiring attitudes either superior or inferior to those around us. We know that <u>living in an imperfect world will help us to appreciate the true meaning of perfection.</u> We ask for courage and humility before our journey into another life. As *we grow in awareness so will the quality of our existence. This is how we are tested. Passing this test is our destiny."*

BOOK 3
What All That Means for Us
(Everybody Wants to Go to "Heaven")

Chapter 12
Highlights from These Discoveries

What does this new paradigm, revealed to us through the hypnotic regressions originated by Michael Newton, tell us that radically differentiates it from the past? What are the most important takeaways that distinguish it from past thoughts and perspectives, standing to radically change human thought about life and existence?

1. **We are magnificent beings on a path to being incredibly united with the All-Loving Consciousness.** I always cringe when I hear the hymn *Amazing Grace* play: *"Amazing grace! How sweet the sound, that saved a WRETCH like me."* No! Many people love those words and practically swoon over the "beauty" of that song. Rather, All-Loving Consciousness does not think of its individuated manifestations as "wretches." It thinks of us as unconditionally loved and most beautiful. Calling humans "wretches" is far, far, FAR away from an All-Loving Awareness (i.e., "God") concept.

1. **The process of growth and fulfillment is so much larger, so much more complicated, and so much more rewarding than we ever possibly dreamed it could be under past philosophical, moral, and theological thinking.** Life Between Lives, where we truly come from when we drop into this physical world from time to time is radically different from our physical life here. On this planet, we are only capable of a miniscule portion of what our soul is capable.

1. **We are *NOT* victims. We choose life's challenges.** Nobody but we ourselves make the final decisions. We have nobody to blame for our life's circumstances, and *everyone* has challenges/problems. We chose all of this ... for our ultimate benefit.

1. **Our everlasting soul is always safe.** It is safe because it exists

WITHIN All-Loving Awareness. Our current body may break, give out on us, and be in danger, but our soul is always safe. Adversity means an opportunity to advance our strength. In fact, our soul is itself *perfect*. Our souls (us) are just not yet *perfectly formed*.

1. **Our eternal home is a place of unmitigated joy, love, peace, humor, and hope.**

Our truest self is our life force, our soul. It merges with the animal-human at birth. Would there be a human race without souls merging with a high form of animal? We don't know because that is a hypothetical question with no evident answer. But probably so. However, our one, true, eternal soul-life is completely and radically different from its existence in human forms.

In the beginning of physical life, the soul and body are two distinct entities. They grow together from before birth to complete melding at about age five or six. Before that, the soul will leave some of its energy behind with the human person and go off somewhere else from time to time. About the time a child is five or six years old, the joining is complete and the soul rarely leaves the body except during sleep, meditation, or under anesthesia. It can't just leave and visit somewhere else as it did so easily during the first few years.

We cannot know our "long future." For one, we cannot see beyond Earth-Level V existences at this point. Secondly, to see into the long future, all the many stages we have to go through beyond Level V and the earthly experiences we are to have would be revealed. That process, those difficult new levels, would most probably crush the hopes of most of us because it would look to be so extraordinarily beyond what we are capable of now. But as we get to each new state, we will be ready for it and not be crushed by the apparently difficult steps to reach there. All is achievable, and most joyful, as we go along in progression.

Chapter 13
A New Perspective ... Way Beyond Past Understanding

"Heaven - everybody wants to go there, but nobody knows what it is ... until now."

That's the title of a small book I wrote in 2011, with a second edition in 2017. It is reprinted here in this chapter with further adjustments and changes. Time does go on, and the growth of understanding progresses! So, I have updated that book and woven it throughout here, incorporating the truths uncovered by Dr. Michael Newton.

This is my own writing, not so much drawing on the words of Dr. Newton but certainly drawing on his monumental findings, and not using the earthly-even more of my conclusions and explanations than previously in this book, and not all are from Dr. Newton. I have tried to give the background and fill in some blanks in a few places where I thought that might be helpful.

Dr. Newton and his nearly 7,000 subjects wrestled with the difficulty of trying to convey a reality on the other side of this life – extraordinarily different than here on Earth – in words and concepts that we use in this life and on this planet which almost don't translate. I have tried not to use those earthly concepts and language to describe the other side. If I failed, and to some degree I am certain that I did, the fault certainly does not lie with Dr. Newton's work. I do believe, however, that I have presented Dr. Newton's findings here in a way that you can digest. They are as true to his reporting as I can get. Here it is, trying for some more of this subject's grandeur, in my own words.

If you find what I have put here to be at least a little intriguing, please read Michal Newton's book *Journey of Souls*. If you like that, read his follow-up book *Destiny of Souls*. You will find them remarkable ... beautiful beyond what I put here. If you liked all of that, keep going. Read *Wisdom of Souls - Case Studies of Life Between Lives from the Michael Newton Institute*, written (in 2019, firth reprinting in 2024) by Ann J. Clark PhD, Karen Joy, Joanne Selinski PhD, and Marilyn Hargreaves.

Let's recap:

Until sometime about the 1980s, humanity could not comprehend that it had recently developed the technology to acquire valid and believable information about Near-Death Experiences (i.e., scientifically sound sociological surveys) nor the methodology for communicating to millions of people at once (i.e., electronic communications). The survey in the 1980s by the Gallup Poll, followed by two similar surveys in the following decade by US News and World Report and by Pew Research, allowed simultaneous tabulation of thousands of subjects on the question of Near-Death Experiences.

The eye-opening results of these inquiries gave us a never-before-seen peek behind the door of the afterlife. It allowed us to stick our heads in and take a quick look around. We loved what we saw.

But at about the same time, something else was going on, something somewhat slower because it entailed one-on-one hypnotic regressions, instead of thousands of responses gathered at once, by another science that was relatively new into a world it did not intend to venture into, happening rather by accident. And then, it took 10 to 20 years of hypnotic regressions, story by story, revelation by revelation, until those findings could be compiled, sorted, and seen from a cohesive whole perspective.

While what we learned from hypnotic regression took a little longer to make its public presentation, it was virtually at the same time as our discovery of Near-Death Experiences. What is a decade or two in a couple million years of human progression and another couple hundred thousand years of actual homo sapiens? Together, the revelation of Near-Death Experiences and hypnotic regression into Life Between Lives is a monumental blockbuster.

Because if Near-Death Experiences gave us a peek behind the Door to Eternity, hypnotic regression into Life Between Lives gives us a nearly full tour of what is our home and eternal life, where we thrive between our brief forays into lives on Earth.

That tour is beauty beyond imagination.

The Breakthrough

Michael Newton, PhD is the father of the science of hypnotic regression into Life Between Lives. He was a hypnotherapist for 10 years before his accidental breakthrough into Life Between Lives, which then became his primary focus for the next 40 years of his professional life. Of course, nothing is "accidental" in the big picture, but it may have seemed that way to Michael Newton because it is not what he was attempting to do. Rather, it was something his subject(s) led him into on their while under hypnosis.

Dr. Newton's first two books on the subject, *Journey of Souls* and *Destiny of Souls* describe this relatively new science of who we are as human beings energized with eternal life forces. Dr. Newton (1931 – 2016) brought humanity the knowledge and the understanding that will ultimately be seen as historically potent as the messages of Jesus, Buddha, Mohammed, or other spiritual masters. It confirms and dramatically expands what those masters were telling us.

At the turn of the 21st century, Dr. Newton founded The Society for Spiritual Regression which, after his death, was later renamed The Newton Institute for Life Between Lives Hypnotherapy (TNI) by his successors to honor him as its founder. TNI now has an ever-growing global network of Life Between Lives therapists. The TNI website (www.newtoninstitute.org) continually brings this science up to date. Its statement that Michael Newton's speeches around the world stunned "assembled groups with the breadth, depth, and robustness of his work" is an understatement. In 2023, the Newton Institute website states that there are about 200 hypnotherapists in 40 countries certified by TNI. (You can probably find one near you on the Newton Institute webpage.)

Past Life Regression hypnotherapy is not the same as Life Between Lives (LBL) hypnotherapy. They are different techniques and practices. Life Between Lives hypnotherapy flows out of and builds upon a hypnotherapist's foundation in Past Life Regression hypnotherapy. LBL therapy requires a skillful process and careful training in which the agreements and contracts made on the other side of this physical life and created between souls – usually between souls who have been together over thousands of years and hundreds of lifetimes – for mutual unique growth opportunity purposes are revealed. The individual led into hypnotic regression and LBL is usually taken into a past life, through the death experience of that life, and into Life Between Lives in a very careful transition. The session itself lasts four to four and a half hours because it cannot be rushed and because there is a lot to discover.

The Revelation

The ability for an individual to see the formative process whereby he/she and other companion souls plan and process the obstacles the soul wishes to encounter in this life usually brings a beautiful but sobering wake-up call in this present life.

The fact that this life and its concomitant personal difficulties are not randomly thrown on us arbitrarily or unfairly, but rather are chosen carefully before we come to this life and the grand purpose of this life, is a shock. But at the same time, it enlightens the individual to fathom that he or she has given themselves a grand opportunity, a winnable set of challenges. We do conclude that we can get through anything – even THIS – if we choose to do so.

The discovery that what an individual thought were the suffocating problems, squeezing the life out of him or her in this life, were the reasons that person came here is incredibly enlightening. They came here to confront, endure, see through, and grow from these problems.

That is both earth-shaking and uplifting. It gives that individual the insight and the renewed power to face life's problems with renewed vigor. Because, unless solved now, we will be back in one or many more lifetimes to confront those potentials for growth and spiritual cleansing again and again and again until we get it. In fact, the individual discovers he or she has probably already been here many lifetimes with just these same problems/opportunities and comes to the conclusion, "If I don't solve these now, when will I?"

Lives on This Planet

Part of the process for the individual to see his or her life purpose here and identify companion souls who are here once again in this life is a deep-seated recognition of the beauty of this world, this planet to which the soul has chosen to come. That understanding of the spectacular attractiveness of this physical environment on this unique planet is a seed planted within the power of hypnotic regression, a recognition that ferments and blooms over time after the session. This is indeed a most remarkably gorgeous place, one to which souls long to return for the enjoyment of that beauty.

At the same time, in the soul world on the other side of this physical life, coming to planet Earth is also known as a difficult journey. The problems encountered here are much tougher than other optional places for soul growth. Here on this planet is an environment where – if used well – soul development can be accomplished faster than in many other environments because the level of difficulty is commensurate with the level of growth. It may take us four or five lifetimes to overcome one little challenge, and it may take hundreds or thousands of lifetimes to move beyond the lessons and growth these physical lifetimes can provide. But that is fast in comparison to other growth environments in other spheres of experience. And, of course, it is but a blink of an eye when shone against the reality of our *eternal* existence.

We have learned from the experiences of thousands who have recounted their Lives Between Lives that there are other planets in this universe to which souls go for growth experiences. Some souls spend all their time in other physical worlds within this universe, experiencing their growth toward perfection there. Some spend all their lifetimes on Earth. Some – very few actually – go back and forth. Some planets are just for soul recreation in between lives, they're just for enjoyment.

Moreover, we have learned through this recent process of hypnotic LBL regression that there are untold other universes beyond our comprehension where souls go for other forms of growth toward their perfection.

(As you can already tell, what has been revealed by the thousands upon thousands of compiled LBL hypnotic regressions has opened humanity up to heretofore unimaginable reality.)

Science tells us that there are 11 dimensions of physical reality. Only four are evident in our universe: up and down, left and right, backward and forward, and time. The other seven dimensions are "tucked under" the physical expression of this universe, unseen to us. Because we cannot experience them, we have absolutely no idea how they might manifest themselves in physical presentations. That is the stuff that other universes are made of. Science tells us of the Multiverse Theory, that there are more universes in existence at this very time than we can comprehend and that the complexity and presentation of them are beyond our comprehension. Are those universes in different "places," or are they all manifested in different ways at the same place but unseen to others like us, for example? We do not know the answer to that question.

However, hypnotic regression to LBL does tell us that our souls have the option and the opportunity to experience those other realms of existence as a part of our yearning movement toward our experienced path to perfection. We just cannot explain or comprehend them because we now live in this body and this universe with these four dimensions, unable to understand or explain whatever is beyond the four dimensions in which we presently exist.

The spiritual science of Life Between Lives hypnotic regression aligns with the physical science of quantum physics. Of course, it has to. There is only one reality.

That One Reality is what has historically been called God: the All in All. But with our new understandings of science and spirituality, the All in All might be more properly termed (it cannot be defined by us) as Loving Consciousness or All-Loving Awareness.

It certainly is not some Entity in the Sky or something "up there" sending down messages to special people, telling them to obey what the Entity in the Sky has told those special messengers or the Entity in the Sky will whack them. That concept – so prevalent for millennia – is gone, quickly moving out, and experiencing its last dying breaths.

Good riddance!

The Purpose of Our Existence

Our existence is composed of many "lives" and the question we often hear, "What is the purpose of my life?" really means "What is the purpose of my eternal existence and my enduring spiritual presence punctuated by the myriad of lives within that personal, eternal, and spiritual existence?"

Human nature gives us that answer, complemented by scientific discoveries and the unfolding knowledge of human/divine components of that nature.

Our Goal is to Become God

That is, our life force, our soul, is innately drawn to forming ourselves to become the absolute fullness of our potential. We are wired to achieve, to grow, and to get beyond. The fullness of potential is the

Source of all existence, that which we call God. We are drawn to it. We are compelled to find our fulfillment in it. We are magnetically attracted to our next greatest step, then our next and our next until we are at that final level of perfection, now experiencing it in its fullness. We are like a gyroscope constantly righting ourselves when we lean the wrong way and constantly pointing ourselves onward. We cannot help ourselves in that regard. We can forget it for a short while, but it inevitably and consistently pops back up.

Of course, for all of us contemplating this subject now, we know we have a long, long, long way to go. We are nowhere near that ultimate perfection. Most of us also understand that our being somewhere toward the back of the Line to Perfection is okay. The process is good. It cannot be rushed. We are where we are going, at our proper pace, and we are good. Everything will come in time. Where we are is a beautiful place. And tomorrow will be even better.

For certain, there are many times when we seem to be going backward, when we want to give up, when it all seems too impossible, and when the challenges just don't seem worth it. However, even if we cannot fathom that in this lifetime, our existence as an individuated part of Divine Perfection rights us like that gyroscope and draws us back to that ultimate goal of our distant perfection.

Chapter 14

What Hypnotic Regressions Tell Us About Fuller Life

The Other Side, Our Spiritual Home

If you haven't read Michael Newton's books yet, let me tell you yet again that they are well worth reading. In fact, I would suggest you shouldn't pass through this life – now that they are available – without reading them. But when you do, you may run into a veneer of a minor problem I had. That is, we can only express things we discover with words we use here and concepts we understand in this life.

Life on the other side of this physical life is substantially different than the lives we lead in this physical world. Lives here are intended to be lived here with all our attendant problems and beauties. We see things THIS way here. We create our world THIS way. We understand things THIS way. We perceive reality THIS way. At the moment, we have no other way.

So, when individuals in hypnotic regression begin to speak about life on the other side, they necessarily have to use human words, human concepts, human perceptions, and human limitations. We have no other way here to speak about things there. So those who tell of Life Between Lives in hypnotic regression use images of locations and processes based on their current, this-world viewpoint.

Does the telling of a room with pillars, or a screen with knobs that move to show movie-like segments of our past life or our future life, and so many other illusions like those, feel like that on the other side, come across as that when there, and explain themselves in those concepts on the other side? I do not know. I suspect that the words, concepts, and images used in hypnotic regression to express life on the other side are not completely true to the experience on the other side because we are not capable of that in the physical bodies and physical experience within which we relate those experiences. They may simply be the best we can do now.

If that is true, and I don't know whether it is or not (perhaps they ARE true to the experience on the other side ... I just don't think so), then we can still draw all the beauty of our new understandings of life on the other side anyway. We have only to look through the current tools used, knowing that the feelings, emotions, hopes, and loving connections are what is most important there. We can empathize with them, learn from them, and grow toward them even if we are using incomplete words, concepts, and images to get there.

As a result, I am not going to use many of the illusions most, if not all, of the subjects used in their recorded hypnotic regressions. I am going to cut to the mystical experience of it all, which I suspect is the reality on the other side and which, for me, makes it more beautiful and even more believable. (Dr. Newton and associates, please forgive me!)

Our Beginning

Even before I learned of what humanity has learned about our individual soul "creation" through LBL regressions, I had a personal image I used to help me understand my soul, my life force. It helped me understand how my soul came into being and how it relates to the whole we call "God."

Imagine a fog, the biggest fog you have ever seen. It is so vast that there is no place that it is not, so vast that it is in every nook and cranny everywhere. Imagine that you are driving a car in that fog. Sometimes, it is so thick that you have to open your car door as you drive slowly and look at the lines painted on the street so that you don't drive off the road. Then later, the fog dissipates a bit. Now, it is light enough that you can pick up speed again. Then, it gets to medium thickness and you slow down, but it is still not like it was at its greatest thickness. Then, it gets so thick again that you slow down and open your door to watch the lines and keep your car on course.

But instead of that fog being a vapor, this fog is energy or light. In this analogy, YOU are that individuated *thickness* of light/fog. Somebody else is the next thickness. Each of us is a density of light and energy that has congealed in such a way that it, at one time, achieves self-identity. It comes to see itself as an individual. It knows what it is, but it has no *experience* of that reality ... yet. It (you) exists within and is a part of the Whole (Light/Energy). You ARE an individuated manifestation within the Wholeness of that "Fog" that, in this analogy, is God or Divinity. You always "existed" (because nothing comes into being that was not in being previously/always), but you did not exist in your individuated, self-recognizable form until this point. When your energy came together in a compressed enough manner that you achieved self-recognition, you "came into being" as an *individual*, an individuated manifestation of and within the Wholeness we call "God." You were born as a baby soul.

In the LBL regressions, multiple souls tell of the formation of souls: individuated manifestations of the divine energy form into recognizable entities and see themselves anew. Their formation and awakening are new revelations to them, and those new souls become aware of themselves in a blank slate from a perspective, unlike the souls who have already moved from that state themselves into growth experiences that take them on the journey of perfection that ultimately leads to Oneness with the All That Is. So, these new souls "see" themselves in a separate and new place from the other souls they sense to exist, a different viewpoint from the other souls who have made slightly different paths of progress. In this newness, they are nurtured and loved by other specialized souls whose gift and pleasure it is to nourish and get them ready for their journeys. These more advanced helper souls assist the new souls in understanding their connection to others, sharpening their recognition of their individuality, focusing on their goal of advancement, and getting ready for the great journey ahead.

The first realization of a new soul is profound, deep joy. It is a pervasive feeling that is the hallmark of every soul in its spiritual ("heavenly") home. The soul's natural state is joy. Even when a soul makes its journey to Earth, when it realizes what it is, ***joy will always*** *be the most infallible sign of the presence of Divinity, of All-Loving Awareness.* That is exactly what we are, and it is why joy is so important to nourish here on Earth.

On the other side of physical life, just as here in physical life, every soul is unique. Every soul has its gifts and aspirations that are different from every other soul. There are categories of gifts or vocations such as those who nurture new souls as well as other vocations/gifts we will describe later just as there are human beings here who choose professions they love but which others would not find interesting. We are each different, and we express our differences in our unique personal way, whether we are here or there.

Each of us was once there. That was where we began. That's where we go back to in between lives and it is where we will reside when we are finished with earthly lives. That is the source of our existence, our home. The fact that those of us engaged in physical life now are *here*, in this physical life, means that we have progressed to this point. But, yes, we were all once baby souls. I'll bet we were really cute!

Incarnations on Earth

Even people who believe in reincarnation are often surprised to learn (particularly throough LBL regressive sources) that we not only live many times, we live many *hundreds* of lives and even *thousands*. It appears we are pretty slow learners (slow by our present Earth life standards but normal in the eternal perspective of our ultimate home reality).

On this side of our physical life, we do not overtly remember any past lives. Can you imagine how difficult it would be to get anything at all done if memories of hundreds of lives or more kept coming back? But we do remember it all in our spiritual life when we are away from our physical lives because we have that ability, and many others.

Physical lives are the booster shots within which we grow, change, and mature into more perfect life forces. We are here to create ourselves anew. Creation of our next best self is the difference between physical life and heavenly life. In creation, we exercise that divine trait that cannot be exercised in the environment where we see unmitigated truth, beauty, and perfection. We exercise it because we see it and feel it untarnished and unfiltered in our spiritual home. What we do on the other side is to *learn* from our *experiences* which we get in physical life.

What does "creating" need to exist? It needs something to make it better. We call things that need to be made better "problems." Without problems, we have no challenges. Without problems, we would have no reason to come here, no opportunity to advance our soul's growth. Problems are our greatest gifts.

Most of life seems to be – for most people – the constant quest to avoid problems, to look beyond them, to wait them out, to pretend they don't exist, or to paper them over. Think 401(k)s, paid vacations, health insurance, etc. But the only way to handle problems is to meet them head-on. We handle the problems best by seeing them clearly while at the same time seeing the "Beauty-Beyond," that which we can see with our eyes and by understanding that through them all, we remain perfect with the gift of choosing our best and most loving selves at each of those problematic intersections. And so, despite trying our best to avoid them, we all get slapped up behind the head with problem after problem when we least expect them.

Chapter 15
Living on the Other Side

Back "Home"

When it is time for us to go from this life, an internal alarm sounds. The body recognizes this and stops. The body stopping is called death. But, in reality, death is nothing more than a change in life. What most people find most astonishing, those who believe that physical life is all there is, is that when they "die," they are not dead. They are the same people as before; they keep going.

After a soul dies, it looks back and is amazed that those they loved are sad about their departure. After all, they realize that they will see them again, and again, and again. Sometimes, a new soul wants to stick around for a few more Earth days to observe their funeral and to say goodbye to what they have known. An older soul will go right away to heaven without the delay of a long farewell.

The disease that kills us may be painful, but death itself is not. Death feels like the banana that slips out of the banana peel. And before someone dies, the pain stops.

Sometimes loved ones who have departed this life before us come back to accompany us on our journey back to the other side, although usually it is our guide and we see loved ones later. Have you ever heard someone who is dying say they see their long-dead brother or perhaps many people? Some say the room is crowded, though it looks to the human visitor that the room is empty. When we get to the other side, there are often more waiting there to see us. Although it may not be immediate, we always see important people in our lives (although they may be living in other bodies on Earth at the same time).

If reincarnation can be sequential, it can also be simultaneous. We can be several people at the same time, though most of us do not use that ability. That is because on the other side, there is no such thing as "time." When we come to Earth, we usually only bring about 50% of our energy with us. That means that the other 50% stays behind in our true home. Sometimes, we only bring 20% or 30%, and we misjudge how much we will need. This can produce inadequate judgments in this life and can produce little results. Sometimes we bring too much, 70% or 80%, and we stand the chance of being out of place and knowing more than we need. But sometimes, we do need less or more than usual. We get to decide.

On the other side of this life, what do they see? They see fields of waving flowers, layers of light, and dark color variations. They see haze. They feel a tingling of music, or wind chimes that move with them. They see castle towers in the distance. Some carry the baggage of a difficult life with them until they can adjust to life on the other side that has more tranquility than they have known recently. When they feel this way, they also feel others' thoughts reaching out to them. This can be disorienting for a while.

Those forms of expression that we recognize as coming from this lifetime do not represent objective reality. They are baggage from our most recent deployment on Earth. Later on, we will use other forms of communication and relationships. We also show ourselves to others at this time in ways that we are most used to, though we have many different forms to use. We can manifest many ethereal bodies.

There is a gradually returning sensation going to those who just left Earth when it comes to who they are and what they have been doing on Earth. It all comes as surprising – happily – and quite joyful. They often express, "Oh, how good it is to be back in this beautiful place!" They do not have time to float around in the spiritual world wondering what is going to happen to them.

" … the carry-on luggage of Earth's physical and mental burdens are diminishing for two reasons. First, the evidence of a carefully directed order and harmony in the spirit world has brought back the remembrance of what we left behind before we chose life in physical form. Secondly, there is the overwhelming impact of seeing people we thought we would never meet again after they died on Earth."

(Journey of Souls: Case Studies of Life Between Lives by Michael Newton © 2002 Llewellyn Worldwide, Ltd. 2143 Wooddale Drive, Woodbury, MN 55125.)

We are overjoyed to be home. The lifetimes of the past come tumbling down over us. Old friends and loved ones are there to greet us. There is a lot to catch up on! We quickly forget, for a while, our life on Earth. We may feel this reception is haphazard. But actually, a lot of preparation has happened in preparation for our arrival. Our friends on the other side seem to have known exactly when we were going to arrive and have devised a complicated plan to reintroduce us to our real home, our Life Between Lives. These people who meet us may not be the people who form our intimate family throughout eternity. They are often the people who meant the most to us in the prior life. As we move on, so do many of them. Our guide was the most important planner in all of this.

We don't want to get the impression that we are infallible on the other side. This is not true. We are perfect beings who constantly need more focus. This is the reason for our continual journeys to Earth and elsewhere. We are all we will be, but we have to achieve a form of sharpening our senses, of being able to more completely concentrate our attention on something, on kindling our ability to appreciate what is right in front of us.

After many lifetimes, when we are no longer young souls and when we have been here many times and are now going back again, we no longer need to be greeted by loved ones. Sometimes, we arrive "back home" with no support. This is not haphazard either ... nothing is. While we may feel sorry for these people, they have no qualms about being home and needing no support. They are quite blissful and not in need of a reception committee. In this instance, the guide knows our needs and leaves us alone for a while.

The Displaced Soul

There are two types of tragic, displaced souls. First, it's a soul who has been so damaged by physical anguish and overwhelming problems that he cannot accept he is dead. Second, it's a soul who has had criminal abnormalities while living. In the first case, the soul has given in to temptations in this world and has not used this experience toward his enlightenment, instead giving in to his lesser cravings.

The first entity is an immature soul with unfinished business on this Earth. We call them ghosts. They are not mean and do not mean harm. They are just discontent to the degree that they stay on Earth by their own volition, not even wishing to be seen by their guide. They can eventually be reached and brought to their peace in any number of ways.

In the second case, the things that the soul has done – instead of paving his way for a brighter tomorrow – cause him to forget his home. This is the far more prevalent type, the soul who had done evil acts. This is not by any means the majority, but it is not uncommon. Self-destructive forces arise from within ourselves. We must have enough energy to ward them off. We, as human beings, constantly have this choice of measuring off our divine calling to do good and to help others with our human/animal-like calling to take from others. If we have not brought enough energy with us, we will be less apt to handle these. If we make the wrong decision, we will be less apt to handle them. And the more we go down the wrong trail, the harder it will be for us to get back. Sometimes, it is so difficult that we have to be taken from the mainstream of souls developing.

These souls tend to be young souls. Although some do have a proclivity to do evil by their continued selection of lives of difficulty. They do not go to a different place. There are no other places in heaven. However, they may experience a separation. And, if they are too determined to do evil and hurt others rather than help them, then they are put in isolation for the equivalent of many lifetimes until they eventually get it.

"The key to growth is understanding we are given the ability to make mid-course corrections in our life and having the courage to make necessary changes when what we are doing is not working for us. By conquering fear and taking risks, our karmic pattern adjusts to the effects of new choices. At the end of every life, rather than having a monster waiting to devour our souls, we serve as our most severe critic in front of teacher-guides. This is why karma is both just and merciful. With the help of our spiritual counselors and peers, we decide on the proper mode of justice for our conduct."

(*Journey of Souls: Case Studies of Life Between Lives* by Michael Newton © 2002 Llewellyn Worldwide, Ltd. 2143 Wooddale Drive, Woodbury, MN 55125)

Our Heavenly Journey

Life on the other side is not a resting place. There is work to do. There are inspections of our life to be done. Everything we have done on this Earth is evaluated in great detail, in detailed reconstruction. We do this with others and in concert with our guide and spiritual group.

The ravages of this life consume the soul. When we get back to our home in heaven, one of the first things that happens is that we go through a bath of light. It is a light that gradually draws us in, swirls around us, and bathes our souls. We are bathed and cleansed in this. Old wounds are healed. The younger a soul we are, the more effective the bath is. The more experienced and older we are, the less effect it has on us.

Each body leaves an impression because you are the only person experiencing exactly the impression you are now. No other experience in the universe is just like it. Because you have an eternal journey of such experiences, every soul is different.

Immediately after this bath, you will have a substantive counseling session with your guide. This whole phase of the bath/counseling session is rehabilitative. You can hide nothing from anyone in heaven. In telepathic communication, it is not possible. But not to worry, you won't want to. Nobody is concerned with punishing you or judging you. You will intimately want to understand why you did what you did, but more importantly why you did not. Often, you will find that it was laziness or fear that held you back. You will be interested in determining why you did not move forward, why you did not do the more productive thing, and why you did not reach out in love all so that when you go to do it again, you will make those decisions. After all, you will not be punished. This is the hardest thing for us on Earth to appreciate: that we have no fear of revealing our deepest selves. Nothing is hidden. Nothing is camouflaged. All is revealed and used for good.

But *everybody is held accountable for what they did here.* Words are difficult to describe this. While there is no "judgment," we are nevertheless judged. It is just NOT a judgment colored with "good" or "bad." Everyone is evaluated by how they interpreted and acted upon their life roles. For example, killing one's self is not the ultimate disaster. It just means I have to come back later and face the same thing. It just means I wasted time and feel sad for what I did. But if we kill ourself at the end of our life when we are ready to die anyway, it probably does us no harm.

While in heaven, we have no explicit gender. While we are on Earth, we choose to be the same gender about 75% of the time. Our eternal identity never leaves us when we are on Earth. We do not ever forget who we are, though we do not remember facets of other lives (past lives are too much to overtly carry around). However, a soul can present itself in heaven as a man or a woman if it so chooses. A soul who has done a good job of advancing on Earth returns joyful and full of life. But for others, not so much. We always know who is there with us in heaven and who is elsewhere on this planet or elsewhere not on this planet. Those who are gone for now are a sort of guileless presence. They're not too engaged, but they're just enough to greet us and then settle back.

The test of this world is the extent to which we learn to live without fear. It's to not only *not fear*, it's also to do it in an unencumbered way without inner anger at others. That is truly hard. Some people seem pleasant enough, but they seethe with anger underneath. That is no way to live.

We are not "forgiven." We have to face the fact that we did something or did not do something. We will live to face that situation again in another life. What we do on the other side is already written in the facts of this life. Nothing changes that except for the process of reliving it and gaining further experience in a life to come.

Settling In, at Home

Michael Newton tells us that everyone has a designated place in the spiritual world. We are with a family of friends that we will probably have been with for many eons. There is a familiarity and a sharing of spirit that goes beyond what we experience in this world and with those in our cluster who are generally at the same level of awareness. Beyond these clusters are larger secondary groups whose interaction is much less intimate. These secondary groups are never less than a thousand souls and are often more. It is rare for a soul to have relationships outside of this secondary group for they don't need it. Everything is taken care of within that secondary group.

Every spirit has color. Color is always the way to determine the level of attainment a person has reached, although there is no embarrassment at not being higher yet. It is never taken as a put-down not to be as far along as another. It is like children who consider it quite normal not to be older yet. The soul starts out white or gray and then moves up through shades of red, yellow, and blue. A few have greenish hues mixed with yellow or blue. Souls gather light as they develop, and this light radiates out a density, form, and color that is reflected in our innate ability to understand and perceive. The light reflects not only our ability to regenerate ourselves but also our ability to heal others. Those two characteristics go hand in hand.

We cannot equate advanced souls with their station on Earth. Usually, the more advanced person has a humble lifestyle here. And just as often, the newer soul has a more advanced lifestyle.

It is important to note that once a person has been assigned a peer group, that soul never leaves the group. He may be taken aside for further classes about a subject that only he is good at and he may form another group with others because he is ahead of or behind her original group. But they never leave that original group.

Chapter 16
Itches

The Source of Our Conflicts on Earth

In heaven, we are *perfect*. But the greatest majority of us are not fully formed. We may not have clarity of purpose or vision yet. We may not appreciate all that is at our disposal. And yet, we are perfect.

We come to Earth and enter the *human* body. That human body would probably have been physiologically the same whether or not our soul had inhabited it. And that human body is the result of evolution. It is the product of dog-eat-dog, survival of the fittest, self-protection, and self-aggrandizement. The human side of our nature has as its DNA the component that tells us to do anything/everything to get power to protect ourselves, to do what we must to overcome others, and to accumulate possessions that will protect us against others. That is our human nature, and it is not evil. It just *is*.

Out of that DNA flows all the secondary consequences: killing others, lying, stealing, taking someone else's spouse, and whatever it takes to get ahead. It is not evil. It is our human nature.

When our perfect soul indwells in a human body with those strong proclivities for self-preservation, conflict is natural. That is what we are here for: to learn that it is better to be kind to someone (our divine self, speaking) than to disregard him or her or to abuse him or her (our human self, speaking). Therein lies the difficulty of human life. We must learn to love rather than to hate. We must give our lives for others rather than protect just ourselves.

Whenever our divine nature overcomes our human nature, we have an "Ah hah!" moment that lasts.

Again, That Incomprehensible Source

"Life Between Lives" is an imperfect description of the thoroughness, the all-encompassing nature of our studies about life and its resources, and the fact that our real life is over there on the other side. Our sojourns to Earth – or any other planet – are but transitory in a comprehensive masterpiece.

The Earth is insecure. It is a place of great resentment of others and much fear yet to be overcome. There are too many people (we really are presently ruining the Earth), and we haven't figured out what to do about that. Yet it is a world of passion and bravery. We *want* to exceed. We desire to make it better. We look for ways to work together.

Our galaxy has more than 200 billion star/suns. The Hubble telescope discovered that there are about a trillion galaxies. That means approximately 200 billion trillion suns with many of them having planets. Imagine the possibilities! And modern physics tells us that there are 11 dimensions, of which we are aware of only four. We are incapable of knowing what those other universes are, but we do know that they are so numerous that if we had begun to analyze one for 20 seconds starting from the Big Bang, we would only be done with about 20% of them today.

Quite a collection we have here.

And yet, universes are created things for the use of the spirit world. Their existence is not the ultimate reality nor even the essential one.

The Source is the ultimate selfless being (which we strive to be). That Source is joy, glorious joy. It is as if we are all a part of a massive electrical connection, in which is light. That light is a purplish light that flares out, becoming white at the edges. We exist at the edge of this white light. We blossom as a flower that opens at the edge of the universe. As we grow, we increase the wisdom which makes the source Stronger.

An Itch for Change: Reborn Again

When we are done with this life on Earth, we are ready to leave. Many people do not know if there is life after life, but they are ready to leave regardless. The burdens of an elderly life multiply and there comes a time when every person knows he or she is ready to leave. You often hear from an elderly person that he or she is ready to leave. A younger person doesn't know how anybody could say that when they don't know what is coming next, but it seems to be a universal feeling. When our time has come, we are done.

Then, we arrive back on the other side and there is much to do. People whom we have not seen in a while are there to greet us. We are tired when we arrive, but as we have seen, we go through a series of steps and gradual re-immersion in the beauty of real life. We regain our strength. We stay there, exploring what we did right and what went wrong with our earthly stay. We meet in our group and with others to study how we did what we did and generally reconstitute ourselves. Gradually, we begin to yearn for another life on planet Earth. This is not an easy decision to make. We are, after all, leaving a world of no backbiting and no despair to face once again all those problems we had left behind.

So just what is it that compels us to come back here again? When we get to the spirit world, coming back is about the last thing on our minds. The great desire of every person on Earth is to be appreciated for the beauty and goodness they have. That desire is always delusional to us because we battle those here. However, it is completely fulfilling on the other side where we are loved for exactly who we are. Why would we ever go back?

After the fractures of a past life have been healed through discussion and the joy of our family's total acceptance of us, we fondly begin to remember the joys of Earth. We remember the physical pleasures, the beautiful landscape and vistas, and the forward steps we took when we bested those incarnate instincts. We are one with ourselves in heaven. Then, we can begin to yearn for the chance to do it all over again, to hopefully advance further. Training sessions with our counselors have prepared us for the next life.

Today, there are close to 7.8 billion people on Earth. At the birth of Christ, we estimate that there were around 200 million. In Paleolithic nomadic cultures, a person incarnated probably about thousands of years apart. By the time we had settled into agriculture and steady food, we may have incarnated once every 500 years. Then with the rise in cities, trade, and a more sophisticated form of living, we were incarnating every 200 years. Now, perhaps, it is every 100 years or more often.

Imagine all the physical planets available for souls to incarnate on. Imagine all the souls.

Getting Ready to Go Back

Some souls are not ready to come back to Earth, though they might want to. Their guide is the greatest influence on their future decisions. Some spend a lot of time on Earth to accelerate their growth while some have to spend more time in heaven analyzing it. And just as there are exit interviews when we leave Earth, so too are there interviews to get us ready for the trip back to Earth.

Once a soul has decided to reincarnate again, the next step is to be directed to the place of life selection. That is, they decide when and where they want to go before they select who they want to be. Souls in heaven are not inhibited by time. The past seems no different to them than the future. They can see into the future and what it will bring. Souls go by themselves to the area to study where they want to go. The place of life selection is likened to a huge theater where souls can see themselves in future situations. They love the excitement of choosing the next life. He goes into this large bubble with blank but shimmering walls/screens. Then, they all turn on. He is then given the task of running switches that change the pictures. This is not what might happen. These are pictures of what will happen. He is watching life as it is happening in advance. And you can control the speed with fast-forward, stop, and rewind. You are both in the picture and out of it. You participate in the scenes, and you are controlling the fast-forward and backward action. Of course, the soul with free will will always have the option to change what will happen.

Once a soul has made up his mind from all the choices he has made, the Controllers come into his mind to make sure that is satisfactory. Controllers are simply spirits that watch over the place of life selection. It should be noted that you are probably not going to be coming back to the kind of life you lead now. Rarely do souls choose a similar life because they want a different set of circumstances to set up new choices in life. The exception to this is that a baby who has died early in life often comes back as a later child to the same parents. Both the death of the first child and the birth of the second child are no surprise to the soul, having anticipated them since before birth.

When we leave the place of life selection, we are usually inclined toward one particular life. Now, we have time to mull it over. We have worked on this so far with our guide and our group. We must make the right choice. And as much as we do not want the heavy burden of difficulties that come with this life, we sometimes move from a life of relative ease into a life of great turmoil and pain when we return to catch up to what we have skated through previously. Moreover, each human brain works differently. The soul, which forms a partnership with the human person, brings much to the table. But the essential problems, which the integrated person must face in this life, are all a function of the humanity of the physical body. The soul seeks to elevate the human body and to get it to be receptive to morality, something the human body would just as soon forget altogether.

We are in for many more sessions of looking at options and different problems to solve in our new life before we go. While we leave the place of life selection with one particular life heavily in mind, we can change it. Eventually, though, we come to the time when we are to go to Earth.

Here, we should note that most of us think it is ludicrous that we would choose our parents. Yet that is what we do. Our parents and we make a pact. If we are adopted, we choose those parents just as if we were going to be born to them. For those of us who look back on a life of bad parenting, abandonment, or mistreatment, we should remember that is exactly what we bargained for. Sometimes in life, all the parties involved choose the pain we endure. Parents can choose this in the other world knowing that this is not their natural course. Rather, it is the human bodies we choose that exploit the weakness we are seeking to overcome while providing the opportunity for our children to experience something very difficult. When we can overcome such pain and be forgiving, even becoming grateful for it, we will have alleviated the need to relive that situation again. Our spiritual soul will act differently with each human body we have.

With the human soul, the human being is endowed with grace, insight, and the ability to tap into the universal consciousness. Our soul is always in communion with our higher selves, of which we maintain a portion in heaven. In this way, we can always engender higher thoughts than we would if we were merely a human body.

Although you have probably been assessing yourself throughout this book where you stand in relation to others and at what stage of advancement you are, the fact is that we really cannot tell. Most of us are young souls. We can say that the more you have an even temperament, the more dedicated you are to helping others instead of using that as a veneer for helping yourself, the more advanced you are. But the minute you think about applying that to yourself or other specific individuals, the more off-kilter you are likely to be.

It would seem that as soon as we have decided on who we are going to be in a new life on Earth, the sooner we should get going. But no, not yet. Now, we go to the place of recognition where we prepare diligently for the signs we will be given to recognize the significant other who will have been placed in our path for some fortuitous, monumental decision. We have to be primed to recognize those with whom we plan all of this. While the most important person in our lives may be our spouse, it can be any number of people. And it may last for a week or a lifetime. The time is irrelevant; the impact is the key.

We will have passed a significant milestone if we can come to realize that our happiness is not dependent upon someone else. They affect it, undoubtedly, but they do not cause either complete happiness or the lack of it. People often state that their marriages have caused turmoil or heartbreak without realizing that maybe the purpose of their marriage is to show that life is difficult.

People who will be with us in the next life are both from our intimate group and other groups. We meet them all in the final class as we are picking up the little signs that we will use to identify them on Earth. There are no significant people that we overlook in our preparations, and our signs are not intellectual. They are more gut, more instinctual. Go with your feelings. Clear your mind and just go with what you feel you should do.

For many, another meeting with the Council of Elders is the final step toward going to Earth. This is arranged, as usual, by our guide. The spirit world is an environment of uncanny order, and the Council of Elders may want to emphasize the importance of the signs we have learned and of our goals for the next life. Although they are aware of our entire span of lives, they do not give direct orders. Rather, they cajole, reason, and prod lightly. They respect our goals. They are aware of our weaknesses, and they gently remind us of them to preclude our falling into such traps, though we still might anyway. They stress the benefits of persistence and staying the course.

"Apparently, everyone in a soul group respects the intensely private nature of these proceedings. They all see their individual Council of Elders as godly. The Elders are bathed in bright light and the whole setting has an aura of divinity. A subject put it this way, 'When we are taken into the presence of these superior beings who exist in such a high spiritual realm, it validates our feelings about the source of creation.'"

(Journey of Souls: Case Studies of Life Between Lives by Michael Newton © 2002 Llewellyn Worldwide, Ltd. 2143 Wooddale Drive, Woodbury, MN 55125.)

Another Earthly Life!

Now it is time to go back to Earth. We look around and enjoy the beauty of relative omniscience and of knowing exactly who we are before we take the act of going back and forgetting again. It is difficult in a way, and we say goodbye to our friends. Our guide is with us as we begin to slip away, and we move fast. Somewhere along the way, I am alone. I go through pillows of whiteness, then through folds of silky smooth faster and faster. Everything is blurry, and then it is a long dark tube followed by warmth. I am inside my mother and I am a baby. This was a much faster passage from the spirit world into the Earth than the trip out was.

The physical shock of being born is much greater than the physical shock of dying. We enter the mother's womb at different times depending on circumstances. Sometimes it's very early, sometimes it's at the last minute. When in the womb, babies' souls travel a lot, leaving the womb to go visit friends or places. Once we are born, a solid lock would have been formed between the soul and the human body. Although, if we think about it, we are in essence trapped during human life in the body. We do escape often in sleep, in deep meditation, under anesthesia, or during longer times in the case of brain injury or coma.

Aborted babies are no surprise to the soul. It too had been planned. There is no such thing as "thwarting the will of God." That is never able to happen. Everything, *everything* is planned.

Once a soul attaches to a child, the work of bringing the mind into synchronization begins. They get used to each other as partners. There is slight resistance in the beginning but not from anger or fear. Rather, it's from the DNA of the child. But it is not a conflict, ever. There is a natural flow to the synchronization. Soon, there is but one object. The soul is recognized as a friend and like a twin. There is a melding of the minds and emptiness that is there in the beginning, which the soul can fill in to make the human being whole and fulfilled. The intellect that is there is expanded. The soul may keep on leaving the physical body of the child for short periods of time until he or she is about five or six years of age. Then, they are blended sufficiently such that the soul cannot leave. In the first few years of a baby's life, they have a lot more going on than they are usually given credit for.

Perhaps the greatest challenge we face on Earth is to remember that this is not our real home. When we are born, we are more or less alone. We may seek the attention of others. But compared to our attachments in heaven, where they are real, unfettered by negativity, and immeasurably connected, we are alone here. When we lose track of that, we gravitate toward seeking attachments in the physical world. And that can be a trap that feeds on itself. The answer to why God allows pain here on Earth is that it is our pathway to growth toward personal advancement that we cannot get it any other way. We are blessed to have such opportunities.

Chapter 17
Traditional (Big Time) Misunderstandings/Mistakes

Up until this point, you may have observed that traditional religions, certainly including traditional Christianity, seem to have gotten a lot of the basis of religion wrong. We seem to have gone off track in any number of places. How could this be?

Just as when we were babies, we did not have a job, did not eat too well unaided, could not talk or communicate very well, and even sporadically pooped in our pants. They're pretty elementary "mistakes." But that is alright. None of us look at babies and say, "Horrible creatures; they can't do anything right." Rather, we say, "Beautiful, wonderful babies! Aren't they just perfect? I want to help them become their best selves!"

That is the case with humanity and so it is with our religions. We're learning.

As time has gone on, religions have accumulated their debris and swept it down through the centuries. Only later have we found out "We took that on a hard turn off track" or "That is wrong."

I won't go into all the ways that could have happened. We are where we are. What we have to ask is, "What has Loving Consciousness, or God, revealed to me that I know to be true? What does this mean for me?" We are where we are because the universe and all in it have been presented to us in the form and place that we are ready for. It is a fast-moving glacial pace, just perfect for where we are now.

Let's correct a few of those misunderstandings now and see if we can right this ship.

Carnal Desires (Sex)

One wonders how (Saint) Augustine could have gotten so off track that he blamed carnal desire – a gift of God! – for all of our most substantive problems and that from which all problems flow. Carnal desires are pleasures (nothing wrong with pleasures, we should be given some to offset the difficulties we will always find in this plane) that enhance our enjoyment of this life. Clear your mind of all this riffraff, all this debris floating down since before the time of Augustine. Thank God for these beauties and joys with which we can enjoy aspects of this life. We get it ALL!

The only thing we have to concern ourselves with, in the realm of sex, is to not hurt the other while engaged in sex. Of course, this encompasses a tremendous amount of considerations and complexity. Pregnancy and its ramifications, sexually transmitted diseases, the possible lack of maturity and understanding on the part of our potential sexual partner, the possibility of our harming the other for a lifetime, and all similar present human dangers – all of these are reasons that give us the incentive to proceed with caution, not rush in, and reason out a connection. Thus, it's one of life's biggest challenges and potentially most monumental problems.

We can have long periods of happiness on Earth, particularly if we understand why we are here. We can take anything with knowledge. Beyond that, we at least know that even a lifetime of pain and suffering is but a drop in the bucket of a long, long, long life of happiness on the other side, made even happier because of our brief period of suffering and resultant growth here and the resultant memories of lessons learned. Yet it is ALL one, and there may be other realities going on simultaneously in and around us. We have no idea how vast the realm of this Loving Consciousness is.

Is There Really Any Such Thing as "Evil?"

No, there really is not. Look at it this way. In heaven, in the life where God is The All of it, in this place where there is no beyond, there is no evil. "Evil" can only exist when there is a diminution of fullness, a partial look at what is, an experience as *part* of The All. We are heavenly beings. We live in the realm of the perfect. Our true selves have no experience of evil.

Then we come to Earth. On Earth, we become homo sapiens. Humankind would probably be here even if we did not bring our perfect souls to merge with it. Humankind has its history, its long form of self-creation within the laws of nature. The human part of us is a product of the law of self-preservation. It is as normal for us to be fiercely protective of ourselves as it is for us to breathe. We are the result of the survival of the species. We have it in our DNA to defend ourselves against anything we suspect is a threat to our survival. We are a product of a long line of "us against them."

This animal side of us presents the first "problem" we come here to work on. Our human side is the one that has deeply buried aspects of "I am the one who counts," "I must protect myself," "Whatever I do to protect myself is alright," "What I need to do to keep myself alive is acceptable," and so on. This way of facing existence is not just a general proclivity toward protection. It is rather a profound orientation that conflicts with our divine nature, which has never had the experience of selfishness. It is so profound that it manifests itself in many, many ways.

In general, it can be said that this is the most significant challenge we have in this life. It is the most formidable of all of our problems. It can manifest itself in ways so grave that we astound ourselves with our capacity for selfishness. *And it is that essential challenge that we take on willingly!*

This survival of the species is not really evil. It is just human nature. It is what we get when we come here. It manifests itself in innumerable ways. We can desire to accumulate possessions to ward off weakness that makes us vulnerable. We can be tempted to murder others who may stand in our way. We can want the best-looking spouse and the most possessions to insulate against the vicissitudes of life's possibilities and, subconsciously, propagate the species.

These are not inconsequential effects on our life. They affect everything we do. They are in direct conflict with our divine nature that is constantly telling us that we are good, that there is a better way to do things, that cooperation and not conflict is the way to be, and that we should be kind instead of building a wall around us to protect ourselves from others. Isn't this the basis of our every conflict? Doesn't this exemplify the foundational nature of every problem we have in this life?

And yet, it is *why* we come here. It's to step by step, little by little, and inch by inch confront this dichotomy at every instance. It is to compare our *divine nature,* which tells us about loving others, helping others, and servicing others, to our *human nature,* which tells us about fierce competition and every person for themselves is the way to safeguard others.

But we can only live like this for so long, about 80 to 100 natural years. Then it all becomes too much for us. We have to return home to reconcile it all. We need a breather. A life of constant conflict and turmoil would make us ultimately insane, and a life without it would be worthless.

Then What Is "Sin"?

The concept of sin corrupts our realization of the perfection of our souls, even as we fight to grow those souls while here on Earth. We are here *to make mistakes* and then grow from them into our finer selves.

Of course, we make mistakes, sins, errors, and poor judgments early on. Everybody does. That is the method whereby we come to realize that those poor choices do not represent our best selves and who we truly are at our core. When we realize that – which can take hundreds of lifetimes to realize just one aspect – and try its alternative of a loving and kind choice, then all those mistakes and sins have been our gifts to help us understand most profoundly who we really are.

All that we see is, in a way, an illusion. We are here ONLY for the experiences, and we create nothing that lasts outside of our memories, souls, and reverberations to others.

We humans don't have a full understanding of what consciousness really is, but we do know that if it were sedentary, it would not exist. The *movement of consciousness* is called "energy" from one perspective (science) and "spirit" from another (religious), but it is exactly the same thing. It is the only reality, and everything is individuated manifestations WITHIN it. There is ONLY **ONE**, only God, Loving Consciousness, All-Loving Awareness. Everything that is exists within it as a manifestation of it.

The body is simply the body du jour. It changes its molecules every year, and we can burn the body to change it back into energy in the process. The soul *joins with* the form of the body, which in turn adds the material elements of the body.

What is a soul? We know that consciousness (which is All-Loving Awareness) is all that there is. It is limitless and has no bounds. There is nowhere that it is not. There is nothing that is outside of it because there IS NO "outside of it." So how is a soul then "created?" Well, again, in the continuous movement of this consciousness (this is my theory, not from Dr. Newton), some of it sometimes comes together in a density. At that point, it achieves self-realization. There are no experiences or memories which form character and personality, but at least self-realization is attained. Then it desires to GROW to its full potential. It previously existed, just not in this form. It was collected and individuated. That is how a soul can be "created" when there is never any new "thing" except through thought.

Again, there is no such thing as "sin." Otherwise, the point is well taken that uninterrupted happiness is not possible here. We are here to grow toward something else. Periods of happiness here, however, are quite possible. We have only to look around.

Life may be somewhat arbitrary once we get here, but it is extraordinarily planned out *before* we get here. We are just largely unaware of that fact. We take nothing with us back to our Life Between

Lives except the experiences and memories we have had. We build ourselves.

We can only prepare for life's occurrences as best we can within the present experience. We will NEVER prepare for all challenges at all times anywhere because that is why we are here: to confront *these* new challenges.

God is the MOST SECULAR of any of us – so to speak – because this is the training ground *given to us by Divinity* so that we might make decisions not in our best interest until we learn that the way of love produces greater happiness. Then we change. So this process is a GOOD one. And because it was US who made these decisions, they stick with us and are imbued in our very nature, completely unlike how they would be if some entity just told us to do this or do that. It was God who gave us all of this.

Our Concept of God

"God" is more than we ever imagined. God – more correctly referred to as "Loving Consciousness" or "All-Loving Awareness" – is all that is and all that can be. Everything we see close at hand and billions of light-years away in the heavens is an individuated manifestation of this All-Loving Awareness. We cannot escape that Loving Consciousness expressing itself in literally everything.

And so, we need not worry about complimenting this God weekly at church. We do not have to periodically show up and remind him that we do think he is "the very best," and please don't forget that. It is good if we consider it good for us, but it is no requirement. If God is the All In All, then we are within God all the time. We meet God at every second of our existence, and we are given all that we need at every moment. We are here for a purpose: growth toward becoming that Loving Consciousness. We, of course, will never get there because every human being is constantly growing and adding to the experiences

All. And thank God (no pun intended) that is so. If ⸺ were static, there would become a time many eons hence when we would catch up to it and probably meld into it and self-annihilate, as Buddha had thought.

"In a remarkable underlying message, particularly from advanced subjects, the possibility is held out that the God-oversoul of our universe is on a less-than-perfect level. Thus, complete infallibility is deferred to an even higher divine source.

"From my work, I have come to believe that we live in an imperfect world by design. Earth is one of countless worlds with intelligent beings, each with its own set of imperfections to bring into harmony. Extending this thought further, we might exist as one single-dimensional universe out of many, each having its own creator governing at a different level of proficiency in levels similar to the progression of souls seen in this book. Under this pantheon, the divine being of our particular house would be allowed to govern in His, Her, or Its own way.

"If the souls who go to planets in our universe are the offspring of a parent oversoul who is made wiser by our struggle, then could we have a more divine grandparent who is the absolute God? The concept that our immediate God is still evolving as we are, takes nothing away from an ultimate source of perfection who spawned our God. To my mind, a supreme, perfect God would not lose omnipotence or total control over all creation by allowing for the maturation of less-than-perfect superior offspring. These lesser gods could be allowed to create their own imperfect worlds as a final means of edification so they might join with the ultimate God."

(*Journey of Souls: Case Studies of Life Between Lives* by Michael Newton © 2002 Llewellyn Worldwide, Ltd. 2143 Wooddale Drive, Woodbury, MN 55125.)

We are not hopeless, though many in this world believe that we are. We are not incapable of great things, though most of those great things are unremarkable in this world. But many are seen to be monumental in the next. We are, in fact, perfect divine beings who have more perfection to achieve. We come here to do just that. Our perfect divine nature merges with human nature which is so part of this world that our DNA is replete with selfishness that is not bad but is anathema to our divine nature.

Therein lies the rub. When we succumb to our divine nature and let the divine show us that being kind, helpful, and providing for another is good, we find peace and joy. Such peace and joy are the very products of our divine nature. When we succumb, however, to our human nature that wants everything, pulls the covers over our head, and sees nothing wrong with taking from another because I may have a need, then we are reduced to our selfish, little, and human-only selves.

To have the great gift to know this about ourselves is the greatest gift we can have here on Earth. It is "God's gift" to each of us.

Jesus

Christians all believe that Jesus was God. And he was and he is. But so are all the rest of us. He told us exactly that. He gave us the perfect example. In the Gospel of John, he says, "The Father and I are one." A little later on in that same Gospel, he tells us that all of us are his brothers and sisters. In other words, we too are "one with the Father."

Jesus was indeed the Christ, "the Anointed One," in that he was most probably the consummate embodiment of Divinity to the maximum extent a human being could be at this earthly stage of human growth and existence. As a Level VI (or so it seems logical to believe), he was acutely aware of much more than most of the rest of us were then and are now.

uld put things in their relative place according to their importance. And so, he gave us a blueprint for growth, the very purpose of our journeys on Earth. He taught us how to transform our lives into ones of joy and purpose. He did NOT give us an exact rulebook or set of guidelines to follow in all circumstances. That is one of the reasons why he came into a time when the language he used was not exact. One word could have hundreds of legitimate meanings ... on purpose. And he rarely, if at all, told people what to do. He told stories and asked, "What do you think?" He encouraged self-growth and gave the greatest example of living by the strongest of internal moral codes. *He never abandoned his ideals.*

And he did NOT intend to start an exclusive church. That was Paul's idea, which started right but then got off track as the centuries went by. To the extent that it preserved Jesus' life and teachings throughout the centuries – in contrast to the lives and teachings of other Masters and other Level VIs who have been here – it served that purpose well even if it did go off the tracks and dictate what people must believe and how they must act. Only in these later years are we beginning to see that about Jesus and the church.

If we act like him, NOT doing exactly as he did, but rather following his example of moral goodness (because it works and leads us to faster growth) along with love and care for others (because that is the path to character enrichment which Jesus taught), we will indeed become ever and ever closer to God. That's the deepest desire of our souls.

That is what "catholic" means: universal. If it doesn't work for *everybody*, it cannot be right for the few, much more than even a large tribal religion!

So, it is easy to see what Jesus must really have taught. Does it work for *everybody*, of every religion, of every color and ethnicity, of every sexual persuasion, of every cultural background, and of every educational level?

Jesus appears to have been a Level VI, perhaps even above and way beyond that, someone who comes back just for the benefit of others. We know that he lived and left us a wisdom far beyond what we could come up with, one that we know to be a divine perspective. It is not at all out of place that we have come to establish him as a source of inspiration and admiration beyond others. We are in good shape if we follow him. There are undoubtedly others too who are worthy of being followed, though I could probably not tell you who they were with any certainty because of my own experiences, background, and culture.

Our "Special Relationship" with God

I am not sure God "desires" a special and loving relationship with each of us, but rather always HAS it even if we don't temporarily recognize that reality.

The "relational language of our Hebrew background" also tends to make us think of ourselves as unworthy and sub-par, something God would never view us as. It is impossible for us to be apart or separate from God. We exist WITHIN this All-Loving Awareness and are parts of it. We are therefore immensely beautiful and worthy. If we could see our soul, our Life Force, we would be blown away by its magnificence!

I cannot buy the part that we can choose to "be away from God" or to "be with God." We do not need to acknowledge God in this life or spend time complimenting him and tickling his fancy. Everything we see, breathe, and think about IS God. And all that we need here, we get. We come here to Earth, to this life, to these lives for the experience of making mistakes so that we can more passionately choose that which is better and then grow from that.

God is constantly revealing himself to us, though not usually in words or writings but rather in feelings, appreciation, understanding, and flashes of putting it all together. But we can never fully comprehend God until we BECOME God, an elusive reality always growing beyond our grasp.

Maybe from time to time, it is okay to just forget about God, whom we can never truly escape because we are God's manifestations. After all, we are not here to escape this world but to embrace it while here. Everything we need for this step in our formation is already presented to us.

Moreover, we never need to be "saved," as we are already saved. Rather, we are pulled forward lovingly toward and by God. Christ "within us" is that fragment of Divinity that is in both ourselves and in Jesus, and every other human being as well. We "see Christ" when we see those traits in others and in ourselves. We never actually "meet" Christ the person except in this way.

We live forever *on our way to perfection*, and the journey is a great one.

Chapter 18
Home!

Being in heaven is a release of all the anchors this world and this body have used to tie us down. The release of those anchors *is* this life, the *reason* for this life, and the *method* of encouraging and living the full life of God, which is our existence and which is within. We don't find the object of our quest by getting out of here. We find it by inspecting the gift of this current existence, looking at and into every positive AND negative passageway of the gift called life.

The reason "heaven" is both so little mentioned in the Gospels, and so little understood in this physical existence, is that the mind of Jesus saw no separation between now and then between heaven-here and heaven-there. We create, by our choices and experiences, our vibrational pattern which pulls us toward our place in Life Between Lives. And so, Jesus did not speak of a heaven-afterward, a heaven-reward, or a heaven-prize to be awarded later. Today, many people continue to think of heaven as some sort of prize to come after hurdles/sins conquered, a reward for today's good deeds, or a different "place" to go to. To that extent, they miss Jesus' lived understanding that our end-game goal – regardless of "here" or "there" – is the unfolding through physical experiences of our *complete and recognizable UNION* with the Loving Consciousness that has all the names our religions have given it. We create our vibrations in this life which are the same that we take to the next.

To miss this gargantuan reality is also the reason we so misunderstand what heaven is and why we always look outside ourselves, and in the future, to find it. Heaven is not outside of us, and heaven is not in the future. It is our eternal now to be exposed from within. It is the reaching within to find and use the divine traits we have in the service of others. And in that process, we recognize it as having come from within and being who we truly are.

"The Kingdom of God [i.e., heaven] is within." - Jesus of Nazareth

Heaven is not a place where we are going after we meet certain criteria. It is a state of being already within us, waiting to emerge in a recognized, understood, and pervasive way through the experiences of this life which we choose, and which are those giving us the experiences of love and being of service to others. This is because there are no "others." There is only the One, Loving Consciousness, out of which we differentiate our uniqueness. We don't recognize this oneness with Divinity now in this lifetime (but it is there, within) because we are busy here accelerating our understanding of this reality.

We are now in this physical plane to slow down, to decrease the rpm of our vibratory energetic pattern, and to temporarily forget the glow of our participation within Divinity. We have done that to gather experiences from this slowed-down, earthly existence of choices. We would then convert these choices into ingrained memories, which will then exist and be remembered (re-membered) eternally.

In earthly existence, we overtly forget the thread of our eternal existence buried deep inside us, all the things that have made us what we are to date, so that we are better able to pay attention to the big job of this life. We don't wish to be distracted from the creation of our unique perspective in this present life by allowing the brilliance of our eternal existence and the joyful fusion of our Oneness with God to drown out the details of now.

Because this earthly existence is a slowed-down, chained-up, and pale reflection of the brilliance from which we had emerged, death – the transition from this life to the fuller life – drops those chains, frees the spirit, and breaks the bondage. Such bondage is good, however, in that it satisfies our need to experience who we are. It is good because we do get to experience "heaven" here. That heaven will be of the same quality but to a much sharper and vivid degree.

In the heavenly experience, that life on the other side, we are fully aware of *all* the experiences and memories of our unique journey through time and space in which we were able to choose both who we are and who we are not. Those memories are an indelible shaping of our individuality, an individuality which exists within the Whole, which is Divinity, and is the Loving Spirit. We will retain our uniqueness, the individuality attained throughout all of our voyages into the time/space continuum, which would have been released at the consciousness edges of Divine Presence. Through our interaction with all of "creation" and especially with other spirits in the time/space dimensions, we will have carved ourselves out of the Whole through our myriad selected paths. Those qualities of who we are, made by our individuated spirit imbedded within the Whole, remain as an indefatigable uniqueness forever. We bring all that with us, for that *is* us, into our eternal existence.

This other side is just being closer to the radiance of Loving Consciousness, uninhibited by the anchors we would have thrown out (called "life" on Earth) and which allows us to absorb our feelings without being possessed and blinded by the Beauty of Existence (which we now call Divinity). Aware of our uniqueness, we nevertheless will be recognizably a part of the Whole as the drop in the ocean, the candle in the sun. We will know that we contribute to the Whole and reflect it, but we are not the All of It. We don't need to be. Holographically, we reflect it all.

The brilliance of light, the vibratory patterns of perfect coherence that would sound like magnificent music or cohesive mathematics, and the effusive glow of color and joy – all will illuminate our spirit with radiant benevolent power. Even though we will be individuated, we will pierce through the individuated personalities of other spirit participants within Divinity so that we will be one with them and will take great joy in their individual accomplishments, choices, and earthly experiences. We will be enhanced by those others who have done as we had done: growing in wisdom and grounding in the experience of Loving Consciousness.

EVERYTHING is animated by the breath of Loving Consciousness, or it wouldn't exist.

The soul exists throughout eternity, once having been formed in the Divine process, using many, many, many, MANY bodies throughout its existence. The soul is the reality. The bodies are only the clothes the body wears on a day-to-day basis. But the soul is not itself an "entity." The soul exists WITHIN this All-Loving Awareness and is an expression and a component of it.

And yet, like all things physical that come and go and like how universes peter out after billions upon billions of years (a mere trickle in eternity), the real power is not in the physical creation but in the spiritual recognition that we gleaned over many lifetimes. For example, to make a table, I have to KNOW how to make a table and see it in my memory. When the table is burned, I can always make a new table because the knowledge, the truth of it, is buried and merged with my individual being.

God/Divinity is not present within us. Rather, *we are present within it.*

There Is Only One

Each time we get back to our eternal home, we are ALIVE in the greatest, non-camouflaged, and effusive brilliance that there is. It's beyond words, beyond concepts, and beyond comprehension. We bask in creative energy while drenched in the waterfall of pure existence. We are saturated in the Light of Astonishing Being. There's always more to discover, more with which to be permeated. And it's all from the unique perspective of the individuated being we would have created as ourselves from our experiential choices in physical life.

There is interest, fascination, discovery, and learning because we are one with an array of billions of spirit souls, each of which is a magnificent compilation of choices, experiences, stories, and perspectives. It is our historical experiences through the journeys of physical life that enable us to appreciate the brilliance of heaven ("Closeness to Loving Consciousness") to the fullest.

That is the glory of it all. The glory of who we are. The wonder of our eventual and always home. It's the ground of our being. The substance of All That Is.

It is your home, your Life Between Lives ... and it is you.

A Final Thought

Life Between Lives is a quantum leap beyond our flailing around with our human minds, logic, and conclusions no matter how deep, how profound, how mystical, or how intricate those thought processes might have seemed to us. (Sorry Plato, Aristotle, Paul, Augustine, Aquinas, and all you other remarkable philosophers/theologians who kept us pointed in the right direction with relatively little to work with, for these thousands of years.) It literally fell to Michael Newton – at the right time in evolutionary history – to reveal to us the underpinnings of life and existence far beyond the mere physical attributes and mental wanderings of this universe, and on this planet.

All of us cannot live with these profound understandings in front of our minds at all times, of course. We are, after all, human. We have work to do HERE. But being aware of them, holding them in the treasure chest at the back of our minds, can bring enormous comfort and a renewed purpose when we have to draw them out and realize all over again just who we are. Aren't we lucky to be living in a time when these insights come forth?

JAMES H. BURCH

Jim was a real estate developer from the mid-1970s until the early 2000s involved in a myriad of successful real estate projects. Among many of these representative projects was *National Harbor*. Jim was the original developer of this 240-acre Washington, DC development with 1½ miles of Beltway frontage and 1¼ miles of Potomac River Frontage. It took 4½ years to get unanimous county zoning approval (all other zoning attempts had failed for 30 years), access to the waterfront through federal property, giving the density needed (lobbying to successfully pass a bill through Congress, passing federal land to the county park authority, where a reciprocal agreement was already in place for use of the park and direct access allowing higher density), and direct access to the site from the intersection of two interstate highways (I-295 and I-95), and overturning an earlier written refusal by the state to allow interstate highway access. It is one of the largest single private project ever created in metropolitan Washington, DC. He is now working on similar, though smaller, real estate projects.

After his nine years in a Catholic seminary, from 1965 through 1970 as a young man Jim Burch worked for the federal government's Office of Economic Opportunity ("War on Poverty"). His primary responsibility was traveling to the poorest parts of the country, evaluating and revising Community Action Agency programs, and hiring and supervising on-site specialists. His work took him into all the myriad manifestations of poverty. From 1971 through 1972, he consulted anti-hunger and malnutrition programs on Indian reservations and throughout U.S. migrant streams. He also visited 38 states, analyzing poverty programs and making recommendations for improvements in programs and federal legislation. He held the record for many years (maybe still) for the most VISTA Volunteers recruited in a day.

Jim later worked as a volunteer for Robert Kennedy's presidential campaign. In 1969, he took a leave of absence from his job to serve as a speechwriter and issues coordinator for Henry Howell who was running for Governor of Virginia. Later, he took another year off to serve as state campaign manager for Clive DuVal's U.S. Senate challenge to Harry Byrd in Virginia. In 1973, he served as first press secretary for U.S. Senator, later President, Joe Biden. Since then, he has retained an active interest in politics.

Though married, Jim was ordained a Catholic priest in 1996 and a Catholic bishop in 2002. He officiates many funerals and baptisms and has celebrated more than 3,000 marriages. All of his work is based on the belief that God loves everyone equally and unequivocally and that all people are basically the same, created within Loving Consciousness. He has a B.A. in Philosophy and Graduate Studies in Sociology and International Law. He has also been a lecturer and participant on numerous panels and is an author of many articles on business, spirituality, poverty, real estate, politics, and international trade.

His 16 books are available at www.JamesHBurch.com[1] and, except for one, are all of a spiritual perspective.

He was the president and founding chairman of the World Trade Center, in Washington, D.C., and ran that organization for two years

---

1. http://www.JamesHBurch.com

by participating in the movement of Washington, DC from a sleepy international trader to more active international participation.

Jim is married to Patty Burch, a nurse. They have 5 children, 13 grandchildren, and (as of this writing) one great-grandchild.

*(**Dr. Nicholas G. Brogno,** Jim Burch's friend and light collaborator on this book, is a nationally board-certified school psychologist who practiced in Pennsylvania. He retired in 2011 with 29 years of experience in the field of school psychology. He is currently a private consultant.)*

Did you love *The Origin and Destiny of ME - new insight into life between lives*? Then you should read *Beyond Mortal: The New New Testament*[2] by Jesus and the Original Authors!

BEYOND MORTAL
THE NEW NEW TESTAMENT [3]

The main question about this book is whether or not Jesus *can* give us a new edition of *his* New Testament. If you don't believe Jesus has the power to do that you should stop right here. If you are willing to consider that possibility, you might open this *New* New Testament at a couple of random places and read it. If it sounds and feels like something Jesus would want you to read, then please do so. The scribe who wrote this down takes no credit for its content since he firmly believes what he heard and wrote down came from Jesus.

Jesus didn't come to the learned and wise but to the common people, like those he chose to be his Apostles. You will find a few

---

2. https://books2read.com/u/4jOPk5

3. https://books2read.com/u/4jOPk5

quotes below from ordinary people who have read what you have in your hands. Their belief systems are noted merely to show how Jesus' teachings continue to transcend all religious, spiritual, cultural, and human barriers.

Quotes from those who have read the *New* New Testament

"Exactly what Jesus would say if he came to earth again! Perhaps *this* is how he will come again."

- Christian Person.

"What Christians have been seeking for centuries. Literally millions will love it."

- Catholic Bishop.

"Poetry for my soul."

- Protestant Minister

"Speechless! I am totally amazed at what is here."

- Person with ties to India and Hinduism.

"Marvelous! My wife and I have read John's Gospel through twice to each

other. Our favorite phrase: 'God's Heart is so big you can't walk out of it.'"

- Couple with a Mormon background.

"Many will find that this book is miraculous, since Jesus brings us into the Heart

of God. Once you know that it is really from Jesus and the original authors, you

will undoubtedly find reading it an amazing blessing! It will indeed bring you

closer to Jesus!"

- A Seeker.